Ken Cato **Cato Design**

Foreword by
Massimo Vignelli

Cato Design in
association with
Thames and Hudson

First published in Great Britain
in 1995 by Thames and Hudson
Ltd, London
First published in the United States
of America in 1995 by Thames and
Hudson Inc., 500 Fifth Avenue,
New York, New York 10110

Copyright © 1995
Rockport Publishers, Inc.
146 Granite Street
Rockport, Massachusetts
01966

British Library Cataloguing-in-
Publication Data
A catalogue record for this book is
available from the British Library
ISBN 0-500-09248-6
Library of Congress Catalog Card
Number 94-61692

Printed and bound in Singapore

4   **A sincere thank you.** Ken Cato

There are so many people to be acknowledged and thanked. Although my name is on the door, it is those who have worked with me throughout the years who deserve much of the credit for the company's success. So much of it has come from working with people who share common goals: the pursuit of excellence, the love of design, and the profound realization that good design improves the quality of our lives. Their talent, energy, and dedication are the vital ingredients in both the growth of the company and the continuing search for higher standards. The work contained in this book is not the work of one person; it is the accumulated achievement of the people known as Cato Design Inc. And it is them I thank from the bottom of my heart for their talent and support in making the company what it is today.

Illustration from the JV6 wine label which was a joint venture among six partners. T'Gallant Wines, Australia

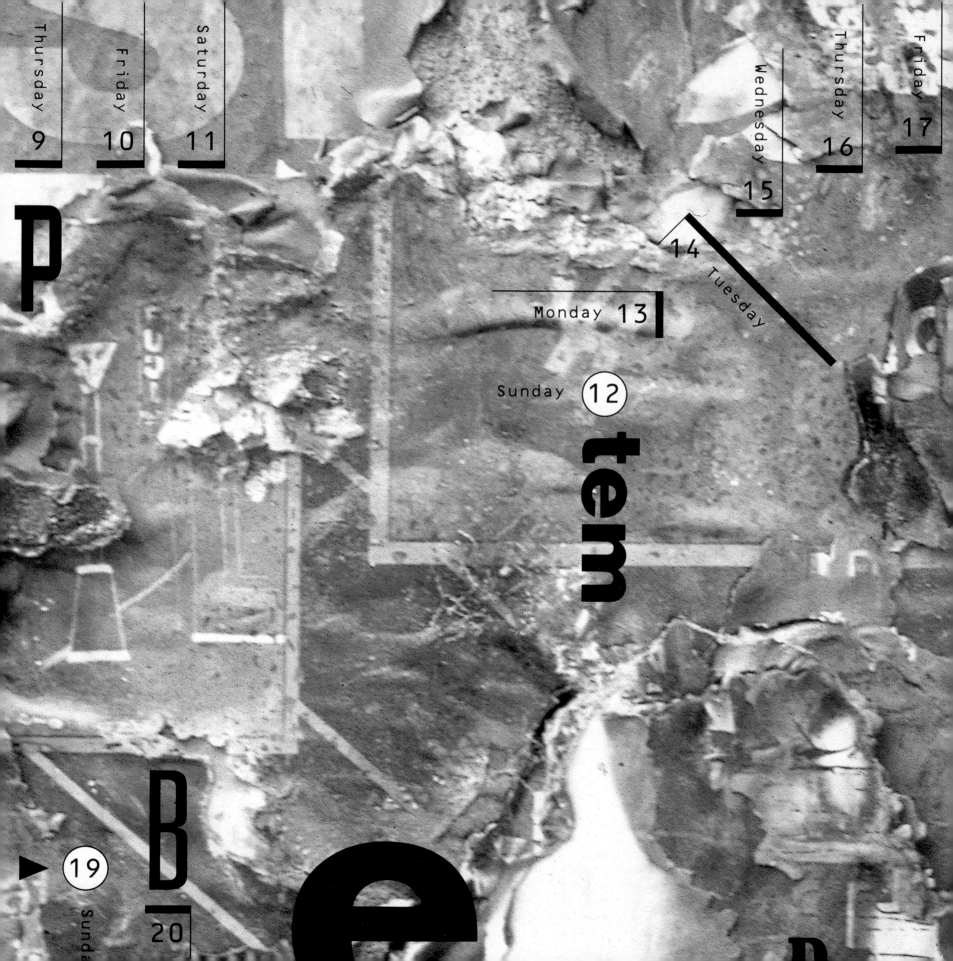

In design circles around the world, the Australian designer Ken Cato is admired for his signature style of integrated visual communications. The winner of numerous international design awards and honors, Cato is the principal of the Southern Hemisphere's largest design company.

The Melbourne-based company has grown to include offices in Singapore, Tokyo, Hong Kong, Jakarta, Buenos Aires, Sydney, Perth, Taipei, and London. Cato's philosophy of design emphasizes an international perspective combined with the search for a broader visual language of design. This holistic approach has created strong, synergistic solutions for clients and has been celebrated for producing positive, tangible results. Since he appeared on the design scene in 1968, Cato always aimed to keep himself and his work contemporary, and to challenge the notion of what graphic design can accomplish. His interests focus on the transformation of traditional graphic design into new dimensions, creating fascinating multimedia and experimental, idea-driven communications methods.

In 1970, Ken Cato and Terry Hibberd started Cato-Hibberd Design which evolved into Cato Design Inc. As Terry Hibberd recalls, "Our philosophy was to set the highest possible standard of design and final product, and to control everything that went into it. We rented the front room in a terrace house in an inner-city suburb of Melbourne for $20 a week, and hung out our shingle. Money was very tight in those days, and much to our delight, and great relief, business started coming through the door.

"In 1972 Ken had his first taste of internationalism. He visited the major design studios in the United States and Europe. He realized that the company's future lay in the Pacific Basin. The company had grown substantially by 1982 and we both felt we had hit a watershed. Cato wanted to make a serious thrust into the international design scene and I wanted to do what I had always said I wanted to do, retire at forty and become a gentleman farmer. So after twelve great years, Ken turned his sights toward Asia. He started to put in the spadework, time, and investment that has resulted in design projects from 25 countries." The head office reflects his energetic and dedicated personality, and is the hub for Cato's work in the Asia-Pacific region. Although Cato's client list is international, Ken prefers to live in Australia, partly because he is a passionate Australian, and partly because he has a strong commitment to help develop the design profession in Australia.

Cato is adamant that design is one of the strongest, yet most ignored business tools an organization has as he maintains, "The driving force behind all business communications should be a central design policy. With this kind of sincere management commitment, the result is inevitably a strong, unified message from the corporation. Once, management underrated the effect of visual components on its audiences. Businesses are now increasingly aware of the number of aspects which are affected by design. However, they still often underestimate the overall amount of money being spent on design-driven components. It is important that management takes control of existing expenditure on design and maximizes the visual aspects of their business." According to Cato, "The power of an identity is a real and measurable corporate tool. It has the potential to influence and attract attention in a world where the space to communicate is contested fiercely. The identity of a company and its products relies on the dynamic presence a company creates in the marketplace by combining every aspect of its operation. I believe strongly in the impact of integrated design. It has always been the aim of Cato Design Inc to provide our clients with the opportunity to integrate all their visual communications. Our aim is to make design pay its way. We have a simple approach to the business of design: Right first, wonderful second."

The studio Takenobu Igarashi

"The first time I visited Australia was during the fall of 1987. There, in a corner of Melbourne's commercial district, I discovered Cato Design Inc, a collection of blue-grey buildings with spacious interiors decorated in subtle monotones. Ken's white office reflects his energetic and dedicated personality. In ideal quiet and harmonious surroundings his designers deal with images, characters, and design. It was then that I realized that the quality of design results from a particular environment, one that is not given but created by continuous effort. The work created by Cato Design Inc over the last 25 years is the product of such an environment. With their devotion to design extended into the workplace, Ken Cato and his staff have created a 'blue-grey box' that generates an atmosphere of excellence and quality. Without a doubt, exciting ideas and designs will continue to spring from this 'box' and fascinate us for years to come."

Close-up of the month of September featured in the 1993 Eurasia Press, Shiro Paper calendar, Singapore.

This book is about one of the best graphic designers in the world. It makes me tremendously happy that it is not about Europe, the land of our great masters, nor about their pupils in America, but about Australia, the center of the Pacific Basin, the center of the next century!

Nobody better than Ken Cato represents the drive and the enthusiasm of our profession. Ken is a very fine designer, a very fine, professional and a very energetic businessman.

A rare combination of all these virtues, Ken is the present and future of the Australian spirit. Those who have not been to Australia cannot truly understand the enormous potential of that continent, nor react to the force that is rumbling under the ground, ready to explode at any time in the next century, when the eye of the storm will be over the Pacific Basin.

Ken Cato is a very disciplined designer who has extended his talent beyond graphic communications because he understands that communication is everything, be it graphic, corporate, packaging, or exhibition design. He is a contemporary designer not because of his style, but because of his attitude. He is a tenacious, determined driver who wants to bring forth his ideas because he is convinced of their quality. He knows that his solution is the best at hand. He moves in an incredibly competitive and tough environment, and knows no barriers when it comes to fighting for quality. The design he produces is powerful and appropriate. He represents a quality of design that goes beyond national boundaries, yet still expresses the energy and vision of Australia. The project for the Olympics represents, perhaps more than any other project, his desire to present the essence and values of Australia and Australians, the intangible qualities that make this country and its people the ideal hosts for such a global event.

In my view his work is the natural progression of an attitude that is complete; Ken considers all aspects of a problem and derives the solution from the content of the problem itself rather than from current trends. He is a designer beyond trends, a designer able to devise brilliant solutions by creatively analyzing the problem at hand. He is one of a select group of designers around the world whose work I respect and admire.

The design of Ken Cato is marked by his understanding of the problem he is working with, by his sense of structure, and his ability to organize information. His visual flair allows him to realize brilliant solutions and beautiful images. His innovative packaging solutions are as packaging should be, seductive and surprising. His work on corporate communication is also full of flair, so much freer than usual but at the same time maintaining his exacting standards.

Ken Cato is an energetic designer committed to quality, with an insatiable ambition to spread the "gospel" of good design throughout the Pacific Basin. He knows that good design is good business, and that is his mission for Asia in the next century. He knows the potential of that mission, and for the last 25 years he has been honing his talents for this great opportunity. He is now ready for the future.

Detail from shopping bag for Rowland at Como Food Hall, Australia.

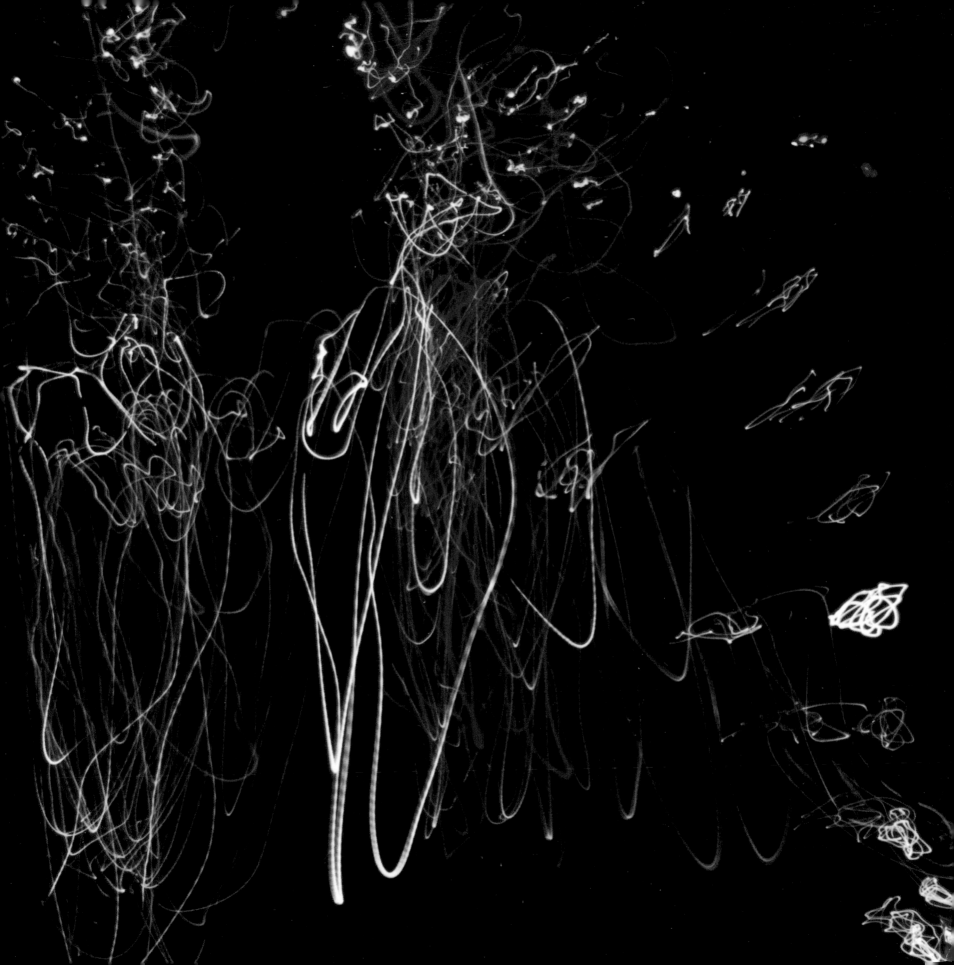

Introduction Michael Vanderbyl

There are talents that cannot be contained by traditional boundaries or definitions. Their creativity overruns the margins. Designer Ken Cato is one of those whose inventive work crosses borders, both literally and metaphorically. His activity as a designer cannot be confined to the outpost continent of Australia, but is emulated and admired internationally. It's not unusual to find him meeting with clients in London on Monday afternoon, lunching in New York on Tuesday, and on his way home to Melbourne that night. Ken sets a remarkable pace and works on a scale matched by the force with which he has pushed the boundaries of graphic design. Ken does it all: two-dimensional graphics are many times extended to signage, event graphics, products and packaging, or interior design, to create integrated communications for his clients.

Ken has been a valued friend for nearly 25 years. We met when still newly hatched designers, investing all our passion and an impossible number of hours in our upstart studios. I was struck first by Ken's wry sense of humor, as dry as the desert outback, then by an unusually acute intelligence and clarity about his intentions as designer. The source of Ken's work is the fusion of craft and ideas – and that has made all the difference. The forcefulness of his personal vision and the skill with which he solves the problems of communication pushes design to the level of art. Ken and I shared drive, conviction, and aspirations as young designers, and it's been my privilege to watch his work achieve the distinction that merits this book. Happily, a great expanse of ocean has not deterred our friendship as we've navigated our individual careers.

It is an honor to introduce this book saluting Ken's achievement. It records 25 years of intensely focused work and may well serve as inspiration to young designers just taking up their pencil – or their mouse. Although Ken's contribution cannot be fully encompassed in these pages, the work here points to the amplification of design as a complete communication and its evolving significance as a cross-cultural, multi-dimensional force in our global, media-saturated world. Ken Cato is evidence that while honoring heritage and history, one need not be confined within it. Slipping the bonds of tradition, he has applied the discipline of design broadly, building a bridge between the worlds of business and art to engage a wide audience. While Ken's address is Australia, his work enriches the world.

Original "torch light" drawings were the basis of the graphics for Aurora and the Light Fantastic Festivals, Australia.

Creating strong identities

A strong identity is a simple way to instantly communicate a corporate or branding strategy. The role of the identity is to visualize the strategy, to enhance the positioning, and to highlight competitive differences. It is remarkable from a design point of view, that so few corporations have a clear, consistent visual identity.

The definition of "identity" in the Oxford Concise Dictionary is "absolute sameness; condition of being a specified person; transformation that leaves an object unchanged". In reality an effective identity needs to have a strong individual look but it also must be flexible enough to respond to a number of situations in a variety of media. A consistent visual identity, with the cumulative and supportive benefits it can bring, is at every organization's disposal. A cohesive, hardworking identity is a valuable commodity that is created; it does not just happen.

Articulating an organization's identity requires a clear understanding of everything from the company's products and services, to its ethos and goals. Yet very few companies articulate their strategies in a consistent manner. It is often difficult to pin down an organization's mission, vision, culture, and purpose. Who is the company? What does it do? What differentiates this company, especially when the products and services are similar to those of its competitors? What is needed to convey the distinctive attributes and benefits in a truly dynamic way? There is a multitude of visually-based and design-influenced purchases made by a typical organization on a daily basis. "Buying" design can be a terrifying experience for many managers. It is buying the unknown. Business colleges have courses in business management, accounting, legal matters, and marketing, but there are few courses on how to control the visual aspects of business that so greatly affect the performance. In many cases different managers within an organization may oversee a variety of different design projects. And although the managers may perform well individually, without overall coordination the result more often than not is conflicting clutter, and a diffused and ineffective identity. Investing in a designer who understands the potential of the business and the opportunities for visually-based communication can be an effective asset.

A visual identity that works crystallizes and projects the tangible and intangible elements of the corporate strategy therefore enhancing its prominence in the marketplace. It has a broader role to play than a symbol on a letterhead. The visual message needs to sell in seconds, communicating specific advantages and benefits. If the identity is strategically grounded it can be effectively interpreted into a broader visual language producing the impact needed to gain the competitive advantage.

Wrapping up the strategy

Packaging is a long-term investment. It has long since outgrown its purely functional use as protection. With the influx of more and more similar products from a variety of competitors, packaging has become an independent communications vehicle. Rows of supermarket aisles are stacked with products that must speak for themselves. Consumers who are in a hurry make instant purchase decisions based on the packaging graphics or the shape of a bottle. There is no doubt that packaging is one of the strongest influences on the way people think and act at the point-of-purchase. Long after the advertising budget has been spent, the package keeps on selling whether it be a can of soup on the shelf, or a shopping bag from a fashion boutique. Packaging is highly demanding of the designer because of the numerous constraints which can become opportunities. These include technology, display areas, shelf-facings, construction materials, and environmental concerns. Well-designed packaging adds value to a product. The unusual size, configuration, and type of packaging materials can increase consumers' awareness and use of the product. Design can and must add real value as well as communicate the many messages the product has to deliver.

Getting the most from your message

Corporate literature is an important part of an organization's communications package. In most cases it seems to be expensive. It is basically made up of predictable components: brochures; annual reports; and promotional mailers. Very often there is pressure to create pieces to standard international paper sizes to maximize the cut and accommodate standard filing systems. But corporate communications do not have to be dull. Often standard in their structure, it is still possible to break the mould and ask readers to think about the company in a different way. This does not mean being different for the sake of being different. It means using components in an unusual way to make a point. Designers are always looking for different ways to demonstrate or reinforce the company's message. Each piece of corporate literature needs to communicate to important and varied audiences, each of which has a differing agenda and varying expectations of what the organization is about. The designer's role is to interpret a number of aspects of the organization with inspiration and sensitivity, and to visually express the client's needs in a very disciplined medium. Part of this role is to ensure that the client gets maximum worth from the money expended and the materials used. A document does not have to be glossy to be effective. Production techniques are not a substitute for a relevant concept.

Built environment

The decentralization of architecture has led to the involvement of graphic designers in architectural graphics and built environments. This has led to many organizations realizing the unlimited scope and benefits of incorporating their identity or more definable personality into a wider visual communication. The integration of corporate and product-specific messages can be enhanced through signage, interiors, and exterior elements. This integration can strongly influence both audiences inside and outside of the organization. Increasingly, graphic design is enhancing physical space while retaining the strategic benefits of corporate identity. In the last ten years Cato Design Inc has been extremely involved in developing graphic design out of the second dimension into the third dimension, the built environment. This has provided many significant opportunities for collaboration between the different design disciplines. These essentially graphics-based projects range from neon sculptures to aircraft interiors.

 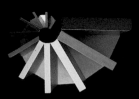 

Arts and events. Eventful projects *In the context of events and exhibitions, design is often an integral part of the environment, and consequently makes up much of the "soul" of the event itself. Events, exhibitions, and entertainment normally encompass a complex tapestry of visual cues, sensory impressions, and cultural aspects.*

To break new ground requires a healthy dose of discarding with tradition, and questioning the accepted is highly permissible. With new technology and materials, graphic design has evolved into adventurous new realms providing vast opportunities limited only by the imagination of the designers who pursue them.

Enterprise Australia.
Symbol for the Australian Quality Awards translated onto trophies and limited edition prints.
(Top left and centre column)

Adelaide Arts Festival symbol, Australia.
Melbourne Lygon Arts Festival, Australia.

Goldie Cato, entertainment organizers, Australia.
Victorian Symphony Orchestra, Australia.
Melbourne Major Events, event contractors, Australia.

Jurong Bird Park.
Identity created for tourist attraction in Singapore, the easily recognized symbol also adapted to promotional items.

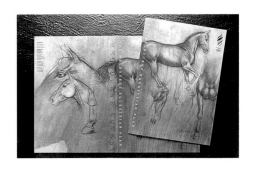

Melbourne Olympic Candidature

Melbourne's bid to host the 1996 Olympic Games in Australia coincided with the 100th anniversary of the Olympics.

As creative director Cato felt that Melbourne's symbol and supporting graphics should reflect the tradition and internationality of the Games.

The Olympic flame was the main inspiration, incorporating the colors of the five continents as depicted in the five Olympic rings. The resulting symbol was immediately identifiable internationally, and easily adapted to three-dimensional graphics.

It was incorporated in the banners and flags used to decorate the city, as well as tee-shirts and many other promotional items.

The bid documents provided details of the city's facilities, attractions, and technical specifications in line with the International Olympic Committee Guidelines.

Three books were produced covering all the information required by the Olympic Federation. Titled "The City", "The Sports", and "The Media", they comprehensively described the city's infrastructure, facilities, and venues.

To make the documents memorable, the top of each book was angled, creating a distinct departure from traditional book structure, and allowing each of the books to be seen instantly on opening the presentation case.

In order to quickly and thoroughly orient the visiting International Olympic Committee Members and Officials, a comprehensive permanent exhibition was created to highlight the city's history, tourist attractions, facilities, and main sporting events.

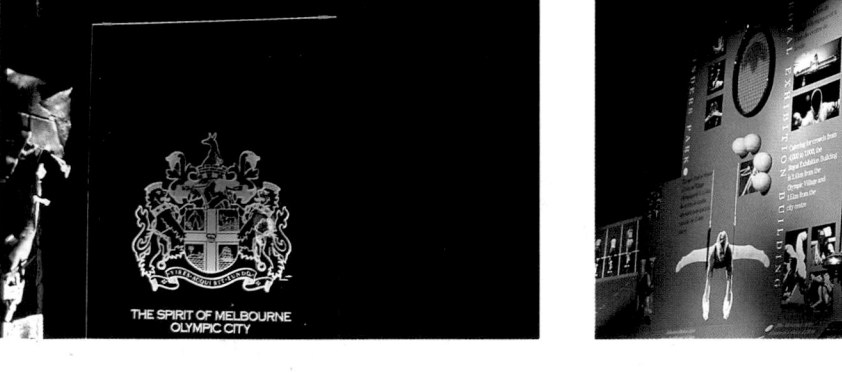

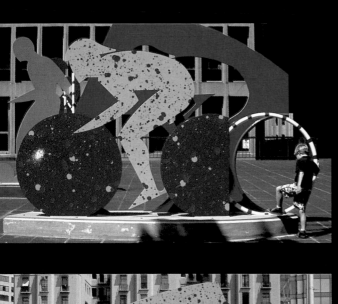

The city decorations included a series of large, freestanding metal sculptures depicting athletes engaged in a variety of sports.

The surfaces were painted in the bright primary colors of the symbol, and spattered many times with "anti-graffiti" paint.

In addition, graphics based on the sculptures were used on the hoardings of building sites in and around the city. Traditional options such as street banners and flags were also used.

Sciceworks / Museum of Victoria

One of the oldest institutions in Victoria, Australia, the museum was established in 1854 during Australia's Gold Rush. However, it outgrew its location in the historic State Library building and was divided into two museums in two locations.

One was named "Scienceworks", a simple way of positioning it as a "working" museum for children. The symbol was designed to work in signage produced from different industrial materials, and for promotional and packaging items, as well as for travelling and permanent exhibitions.

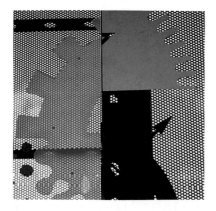

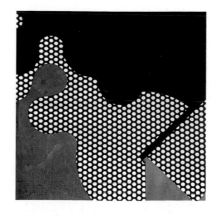

NIGHT LIFE
WHO'S HERE
HOW TO GET ABOUT

KIDABOUT COOLUM QUEENSLAND AUSTRALIA

YPO

Each year the international Young Presidents' Organization holds a number of five-day international universities for its members.

Queensland University needed a special identity to reflect Australia's uniqueness without using the hackneyed boomerang, koala, and kangaroo.

The identity also needed to be flexible enough to cover everything from promotional material and site decoration, right through to the luggage tags.

The design incorporated an Australian color palette and symbols as a means of promotion, and site communication.

Tabaret

A unique network of computerized gaming and wagering outlets in Victoria, Australia. The design strategy included creating a distinctive concept from which multiple outlets could be developed.

The identity had to be flexible enough to be translated through various materials and finishes, depending on the different locations of future outlets.

It was also vital that the interiors reflected the excitement of gaming, whilst projecting a sophisticated environment, sympathetic to the various buildings in which the outlets would eventually be located.

The symbol focused on the bright colors and equipment shapes associated with Tabaret sporting events and betting games.

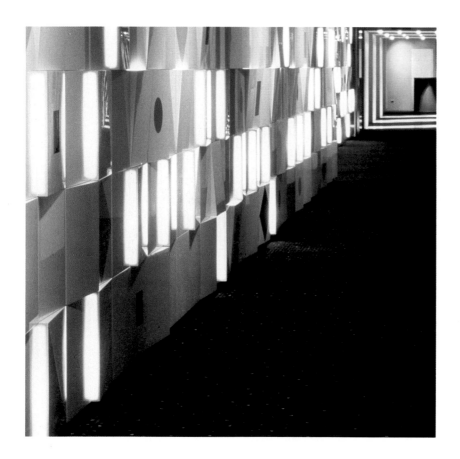

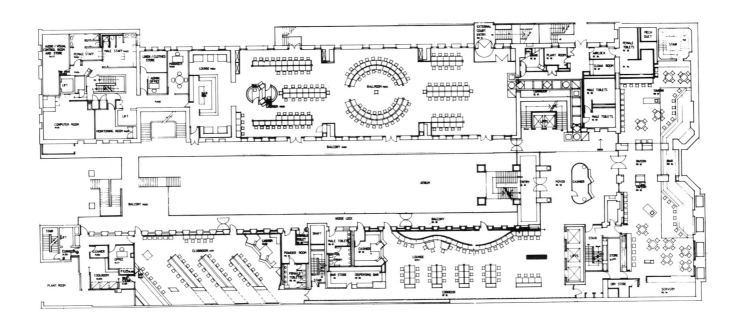

IDEAS Student Conference

The IDEAS (International Designers Educating Australasian Students) conference originated in 1991.

Now held annually in Melbourne, it is internationally aligned with AGI and ICOGRADA.
It now attracts well over 1000 students from as far away as Singapore, Malaysia, and New Zealand.

Six international speakers and prominent Australian designers from different disciplines make presentations at a variety of events.

Cato Design Inc works with a student committee to organize the event.

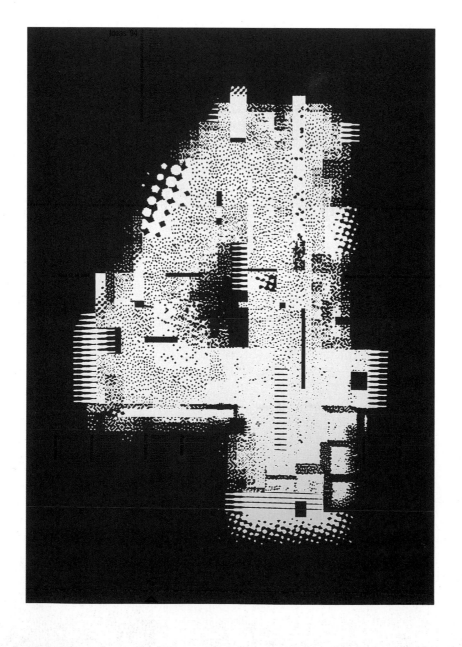

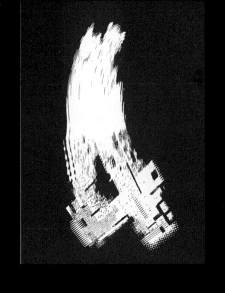

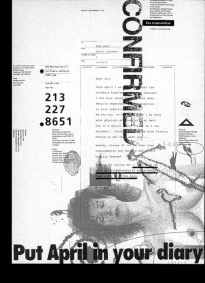

See Fukuda do his tricks

Put April in your diary

Melbourne International Festival

The Festival combines a variety of theater, music, drama, and mixed media art forms. The program is designed to draw people from all age groups and cultures.

The symbol was derived from a theatrical mask transformed into a simple graphic.

It imparts a sense of expectation and intrigue, while clearly communicating the Festival's visual arts content.

Year after year, the different interpretations of the mask have enhanced the mystery and provocative allure of the Festival.

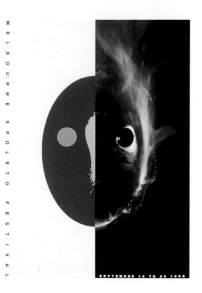

MELBOURNE SPOLETO FESTIVAL

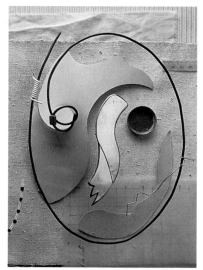

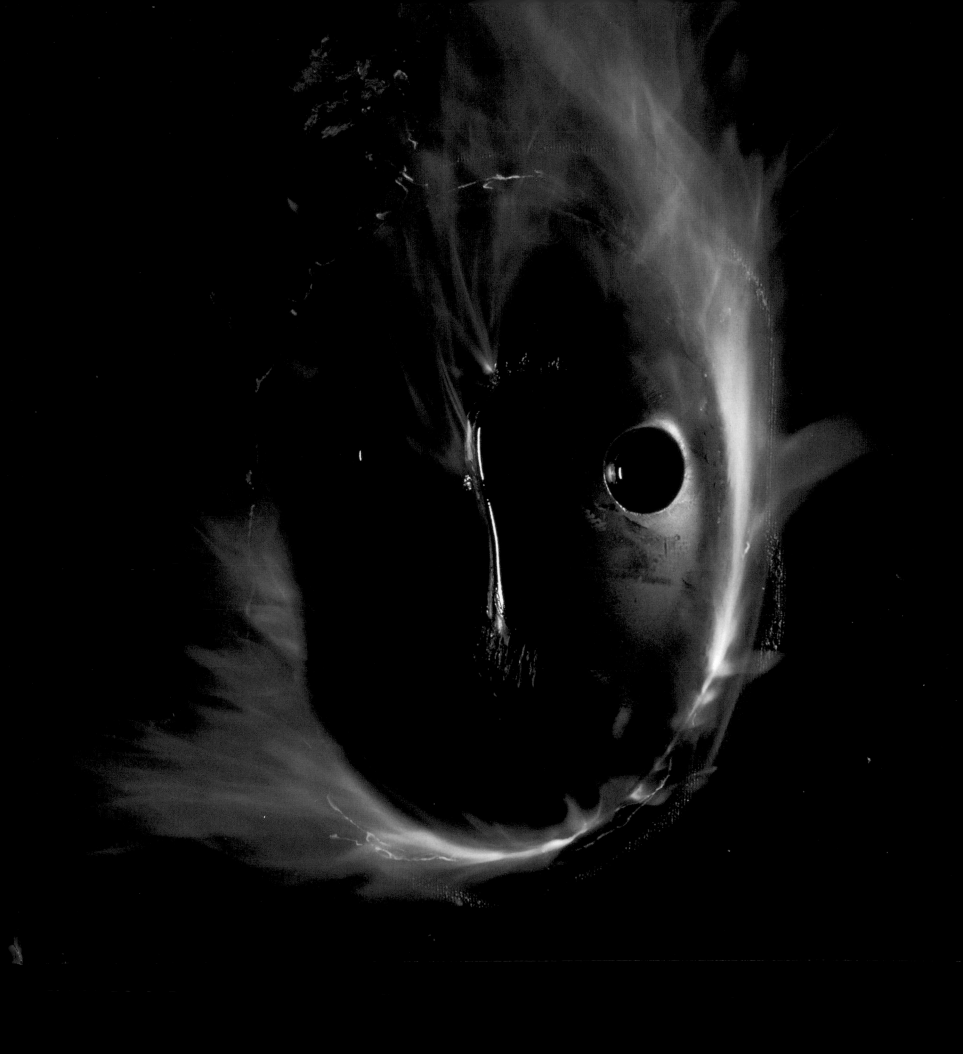

34

Austrade

The design of the "Partner Country" exhibit at the CeBIT 95 in Hanover, Germany, emphasized Australia as the focus of attention at the world's largest information and technology trade fair. The theme, "Intelligent Australia", was translated by technology-related visual cues and human forms.

Intelligent Australia

Austrade

CeBIT 1995

Hannover
Germany

The Victorian Arts Centre

The premier venue for the performing arts in Victoria, Australia, The Victorian Arts Centre is a substantial complex housing theaters, studios, a performing arts museum, reception rooms, restaurants, and bars.

The symbol adopted the center's distinctive landmark spire and utilized it as the unifying element throughout the identity program.

Decorations for the Tenth Anniversary Celebrations of the Victorian Arts Centre utilized a stylized Roman numeral ten and incorporated the distinctive shape of the Victorian Arts Centre building.

The poster design was also adapted to street banners lining the thoroughfare outside the Arts Centre and as a three-storey wall hanging covering the facade of the building.

World Expo '88 was held in Queensland, Australia. Cato's role was to design the identity for the Expo and a number of major projects in and around the site, which hugged the banks of the Brisbane River.

Hand-painted banners featuring graphic interpretations of the tropical flora and fauna for which Queensland is famous, welcomed visitors to the international fair. The butterflies, colorful tropical birds, aquatic shapes, and abstract celestial forms in bright pastels were then adapted for the walls and hoardings used as screens to hide equipment and construction areas.

Sitescaping the Aquacade created opportunities from potential problems. The complex contained a special aquatic theater designed to accommodate a wide range of water activities. The exposed back of each of the three grandstands provided space on which to develop an aquatic graphic and sculptural solution, thus camouflaging the underside of the structure.

A simple painted wave-form extended 40 meters across the top and bottom of the stands. It was connected vertically by a giant kinetic mobile made from pieces of aluminium, representing organic aquatic forms. The largest individual pieces were four meters in length and were harnessed in such a way as to allow them to swivel freely.

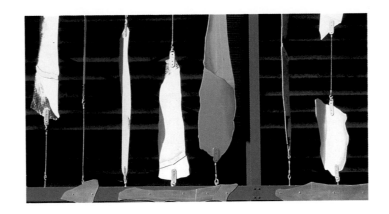

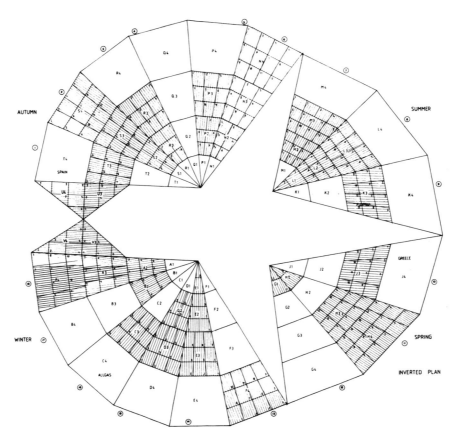

SUMMER

AUTUMN

SPAIN

WINTER

ALLGAS

GREECE

SPRING

INVERTED PLAN

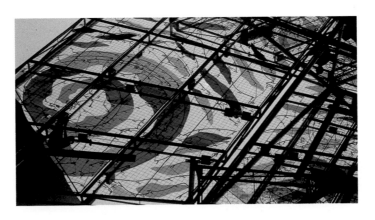

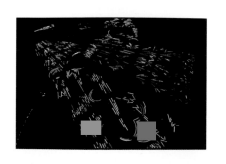
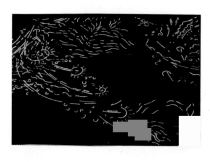

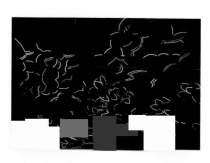

The focal point of World Expo '88 was a highly complex neon ceiling over the pedestrian thoroughfare of Time Square, the center of the Expo site. The ceiling covered three separate pavilions and a three-storey Victorian building. The supporting steel structure was constructed from 180 tons of steel, and supported three levels of neon which were divided into quadrants representing the four seasons.

The overall effect was of a continual change of seasons as each was illuminated in turn. For daytime viewing, colored mesh shapes symbolizing seasonal occurrences were incorporated into the design. The ceiling's core was a reflective silver pyramid which housed the highly sophisticated laser projection system.

The neon ceiling used six kilometers of neon tubing. The fragile neon tubing had to endure extreme weather conditions. The ceiling had a diameter of 72 meters and a circumference of 220 meters. The height ranged from 17 meters to 30 meters. The power supply drew 600 amps through 1200 transformers.

Eleven large neon ground sculptures provided a visual link between the neon ceiling in Time Square, and the pedestrian thoroughfares below. Up to six meters in height, they were based on time-related images such as metronomes, hourglasses, and abstract representations of passing time.

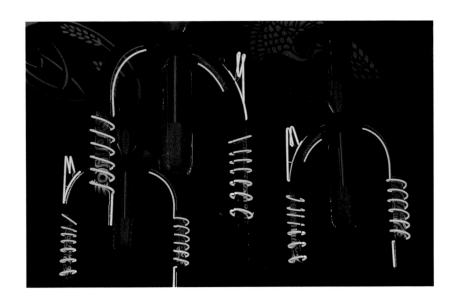

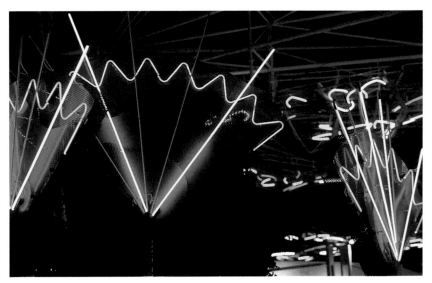

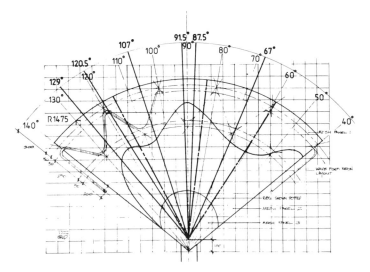

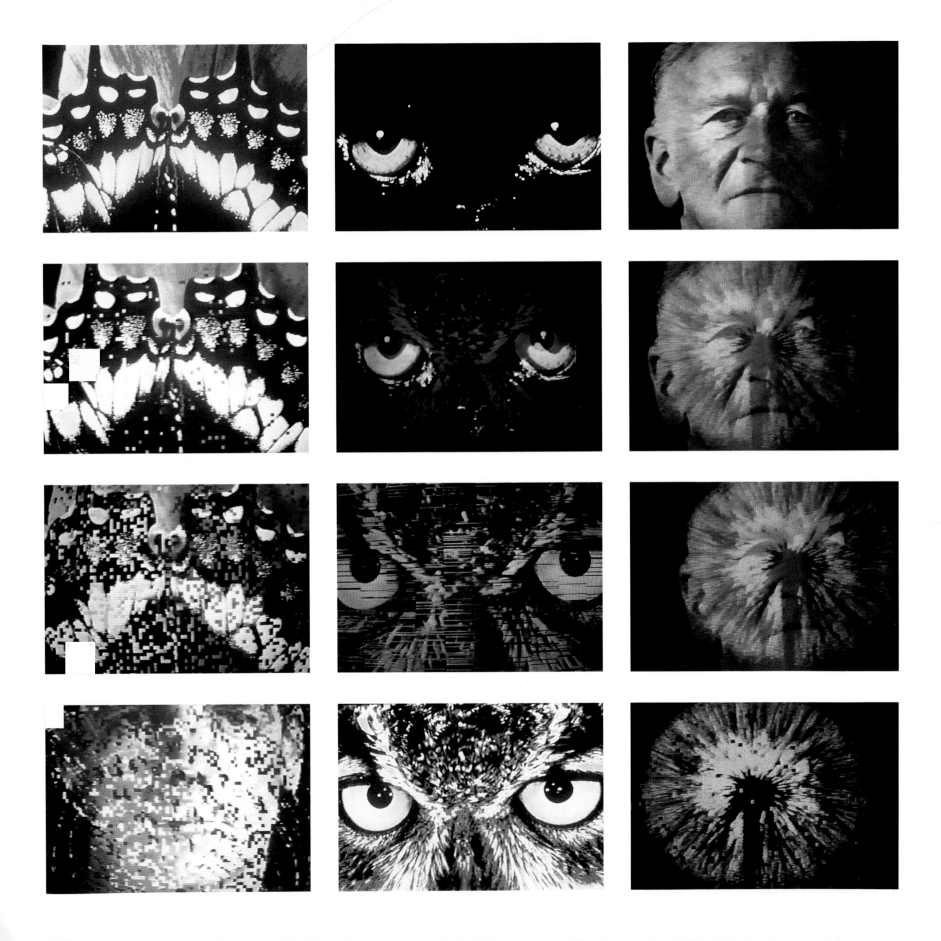

One Australia

According to John Bertrand, leader of the 1995 One Australia America's Cup Challenge, "The challenge is much more than a boat race, it is part of a much greater opportunity for Australia across a broad field of scientific and technical endeavours.

Although the prime objective is to win, the challenge has been structured to develop opportunities and benefits for Australia that will extend long beyond the event in 1995."

Because of the importance and the complexity of the project, a strong identity was needed to instantly create a unified, positive image for One Australia. The One Australia symbol combines an image of strong technological resources with Australian cultural design elements.

Darling Harbour Authority

Aurora is a multicultural festival, held every October in the lead up to the 2000 Olympics in Sydney, Australia. It hosts an impressive array of entertainment from aqua parades and fireworks, to music and food festivals. The identity is based on the dictionary definition of "Aurora" as a "display in the skies of moving streamers, and curtains of light visible at high altitudes and probably caused by streams of charged particles from the sun, passing into the earth's magnetic field".

Darling Harbour Authority
Level 16
2 Market Street Sydney
New South Wales 2000

Telephone (02) 286 0100
Facsimile (02) 286 0199

Aurora

New World Festival

'Aurora – A display
in the skies of moving
streamers, bands, curtains
or arcs of light.'

Darling Harbour

1–9 October 1994

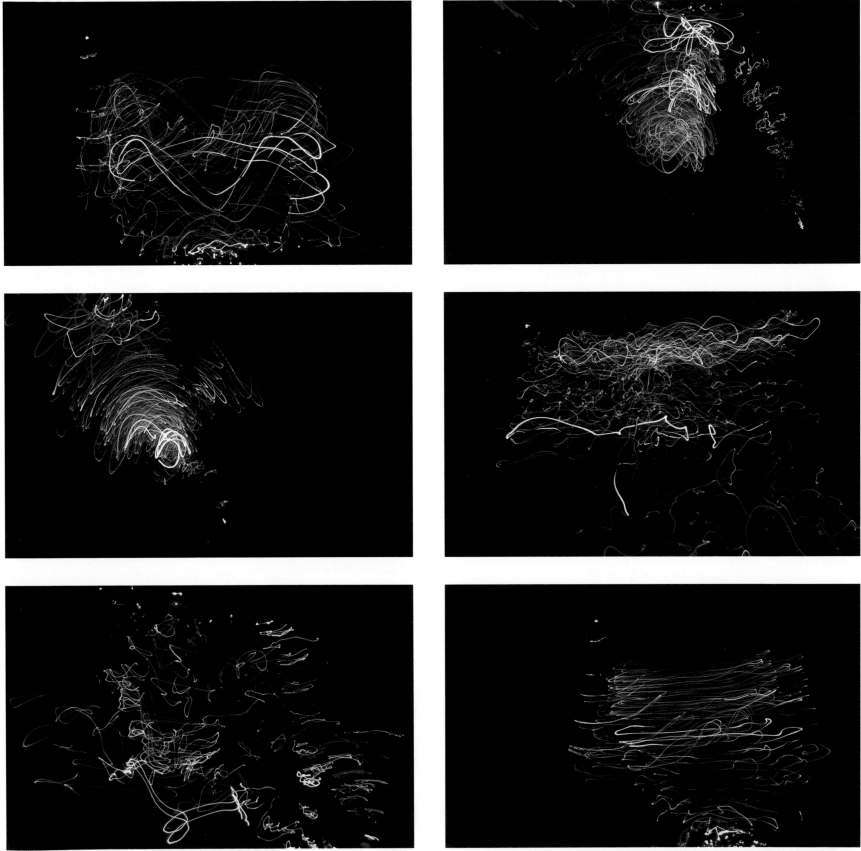

The concept of photographed "torch light" drawings, which were the basis of the graphics for Aurora and the Light Fantastic Festivals, were adapted to banners, brochures, stationery, and media press material.

Macquarie Bank

A new bank which was named after Governor Macquarie, who is considered to be the founder of Australian banking. The symbol was based on Governor Macquarie's innovative idea for producing different denominations of the colonial currency by stamping out the center of silver coins and retaining both pieces.

By adopting the shape of the larger coin (the "holey dollar") a sense of history was established. The corporate colors of silver, black, and grey, and the symbol, were reproduced and integrated throughout all the bank's collateral material, forms, signage, check books, uniforms, and wall fabrics.

Nomura Investor Relations

A member company of Nomura Securities Company group (NIR), a sizable Japanese company specializing in investor relations including planning, consultation, and marketing. (Right hand page)

Symbols for Bank of Singapore, Colonial Mutual Investment Management Limited, Australia, Ultimate Funds Limited, investment company, Australia. (Bottom right hand page)

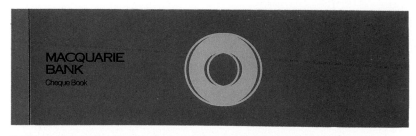

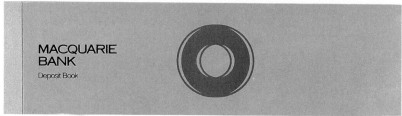

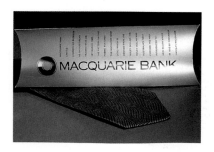

Finance. Investing in design *In the last few years banking and financial institutions worldwide have had to reassess their businesses, and as a result their visual identities. The ambivalent economy, merger mentality, and the development of new banking organizations, have led to a realization that these institutions must actively attract customers just like any other retail or service industry. Financial institutions have had to develop products and services that are tailored to their target groups. From a design point of view, financial institutions are extremely complex, requiring discipline and groundwork to ensure all forms of visual communication are adequately incorporated into the overall identity program. They require systems flexible enough to accommodate documents, thousands of forms and sub-branded products. In many cases subsidiary companies must also be accommodated to position them as part of a group, yet retain certain individual characteristics. The setting up of a long-term implementation program is a crucial part of ensuring strong branding and visual integrity.*

Australia's largest bank undertook the most complex identity and implementation program ever completed in Australia.

From start to launch it took over three and a half years, and included the design of over 5000 items and 2500 outlets, and the education of 48000 employees.

There was a strong fashion element in the designing of passbooks, check books, and credit cards for Bank customers. Employee uniforms were presented to staff in a very stylish fashion magazine format.

The Bank's identity had to be able to extend to its other subsidiaries. The individual identities needed to share family resemblance, yet still retain independence.

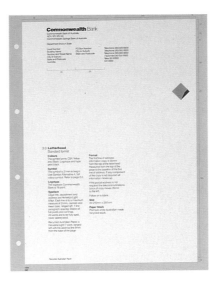

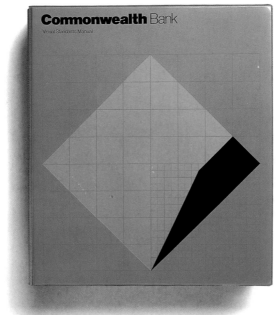

The Bank of Western Australia

Over 100 years the R&I Bank has grown to be the largest financial institution in Western Australia.

The phased implementation of the new corporate identity system involves hundreds of items, ranging from checks, credit cards, and stationery, to branch design. In all, approximately 2000 items were reviewed.

A complete staff wardrobe was created, including a selection of sweaters that were designed in conjunction with Coogi™, makers of distinctive knitwear.

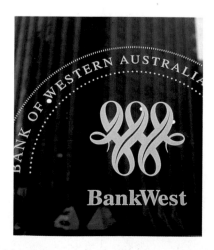

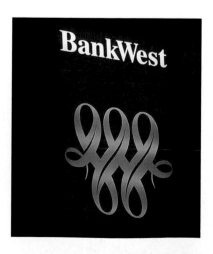

BankWest

The new BankWest identity needed to be contemporary and distinctive, yet still retain some traditional banking values.

Money, bank notes, and security patterns on legal documents were the inspiration for the new symbol and graphics system, which was then adapted to a launch video.

The retail environment. Romancing the consumer

The design of retail stores and packaging ultimately has the very simple function of selling products via brand identity. The difficulty in creating successful retail identities is that retailing activities and products are prone to constant change, and the effective identities need carefully thought out, long-term strategies that accommodate changes without sacrificing the integrity of the identity. The role of the designer is to help ensure retail and brand identities have integrity, and that they also create compelling visual cues which attract customers and enhance marketplace positioning. In reality an identity must accommodate corporate philosophy, retail strategies, guidelines, existing technologies, and production facilities. These things cannot replace a designer's instinct, they are merely challenges to be overcome and tools to be employed in the design process. It is important that intuitive judgments are not overshadowed by technological hiccups. Negative statements are unacceptable to the lateral mind. This attitude opens up possibilities for new production techniques, new packaging materials, new products, and new architectural solutions for the retail environment. Often this increases the number of simple and cost-effective ways of producing powerful pieces of retail design.

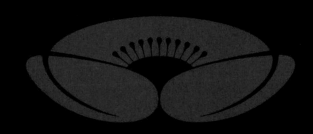

On The Spot, film processing chain, Australia.
Nero's, chain of pizza restaurants, Australia.
Clairol Academy, hairstylists advisory group, Japan.

Econ Minimart, chain of convenience stores, Singapore.
Trading Post, trading company, Singapore.
Weaver & Lock, manufacturers and marketers of soft drinks, Australia.

Neat n' Trim, uniform manufacturers and retailers, Australia.
Meadow Lea, vegetable oil manufacturers, Australia.
Idiom, furniture manufacturer and retailer, Australia.

Poppy King Industries, Australia. The packaging symbol for this highly succesful range of lipsticks was derived from the name of the company's founder, and has international appeal.

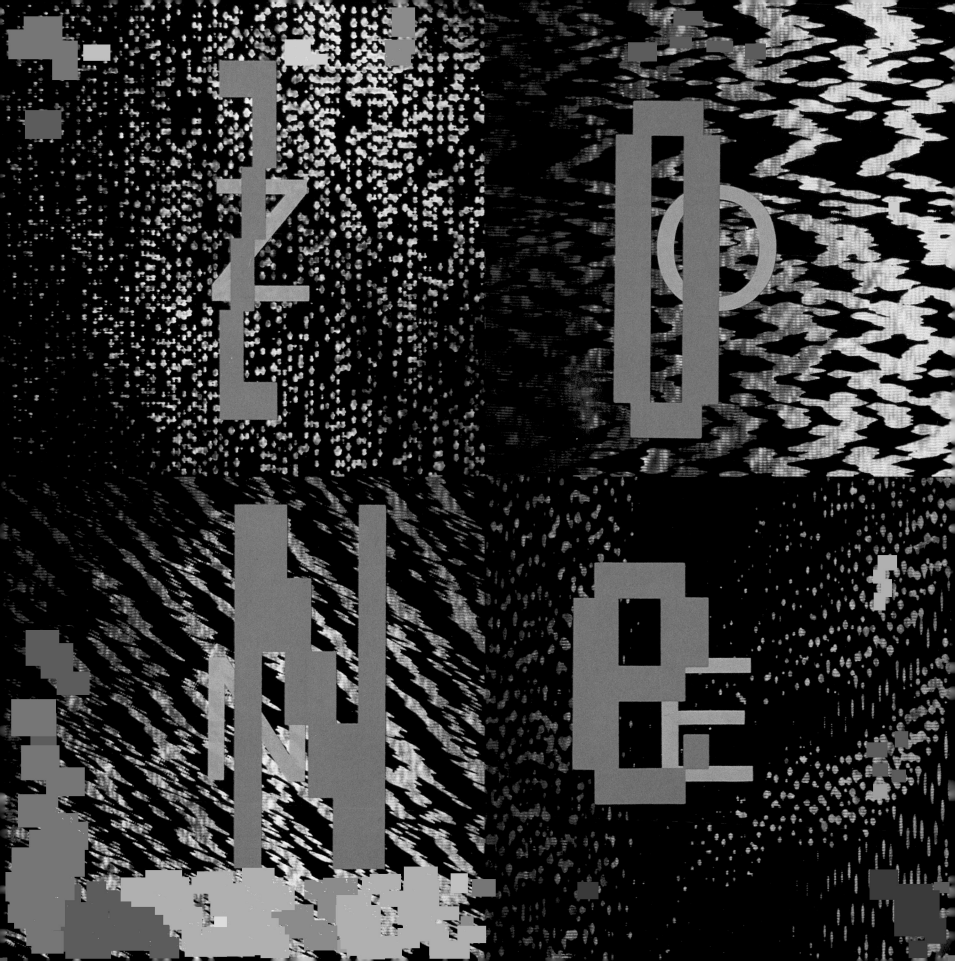

Metro (Private) Limited

Metro, a large Singaporean department store chain, created Zone, a "store-within-a-store" aimed at the international youth market. The visual captured the concept of high tech music videos with electronic-influenced graphics.

The Zone store concept comprised different boutiques including The Nature Company, which sells clothing made from natural fibres, and Footprints, a high fashion shoe store.

Portmans

In the highly competitive fashion world, Portmans, an Australian women's fashion chain, decided to bring its identity up to date. The clean graphics and vibrant colors used in the signage made a strong statement, supported by shopping bags that acted as walking testimonials for the stores.

Rowland Commercial Catering

Rowland at Como was designed as a sophisticated food court with seven different brasseries offering a variety of cuisines.

A new identity, which included packaging, environmental graphics, and signage, was designed to add atmosphere to the area. To complement the architecture, suspended metal signs were hung over outlets, and the graphics and supporting signage were etched onto glass panels.

Palmer Corporation

The trademark of Adele Palmer, one of Australia's most successful fashion designers, is to combine highly textured fabrics to create patterns on patterns, with a dash of strong, plain color for contrast. The bag design highlighted her flair for this, and resulted in packaging that created a fashion statement of its own.

The black and white pattern changed with the season, while the red and blue colors, and logotype remained constant.

Osaka's largest and best-established department store decided to bring a fresh, fashionable look to the store's packaging. This was accomplished by using a freehand brushstroke. To complement the updated bags, dainty silver and white versions of the logotype were also printed on the gift-wrap.

Grace Brothers

The largest department store chain in New South Wales, Australia, required a strong, modern image. The new identity had to be flexible enough to cover a myriad of items, from trucks to store credit cards to paper cups.

The graphic interpretation of the state's flower, the waratah, provided strong visual impact appealing in particular to the predominantly female shoppers. It was critical that the solution was cost-effective, due to the sheer volume of the items.

← Liquor Store

← Entrance

↑ Despatch

Car Park →

Dock ↓

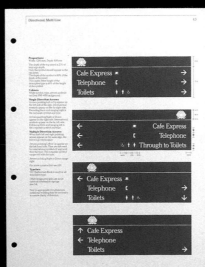

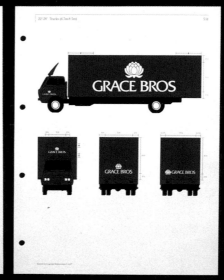

Cafe Express →
Telephone →
Toilets →

Cafe Express ←
Telephone ←
Through to Toilets →

← Cafe Express
Telephone ←
Toilets →

↑ Cafe Express
← Telephone
Toilets →

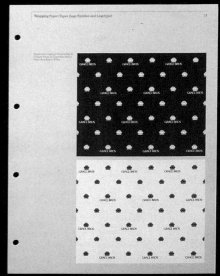

GRACE BROS

GRACE BROS

GRACE BROS

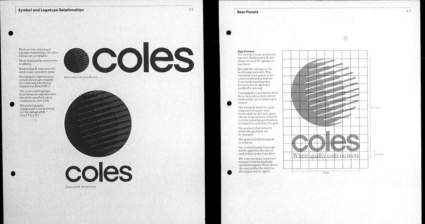

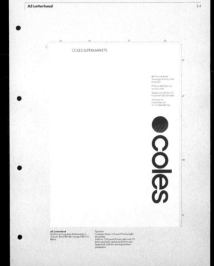

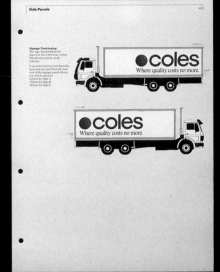

Coles Supermarkets

The expansion of Coles, Australia's largest supermarket chain, led to a number of store categories that blurred the collective image power of the company's 350 plus stores.

The first objective was to simplify their name, and to design the new identity which was used on the store signage, stationery, uniforms, advertising, packaging, and merchandising materials.

The new global symbol provided historical links through strong visual cues to the discarded component of the previous name, New World, and the retention of the color red.

The store interiors were redesigned to enhance the shopping experience. New, focused lighting accentuated the merchandise, and the clean, well-lit end-aisles highlighted the specials.

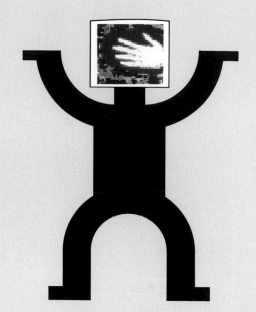

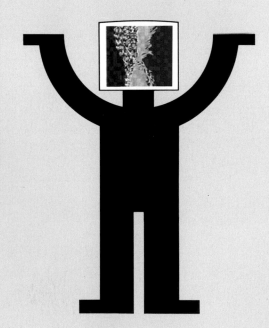

Computer Wiz

A chain of specialty computer shops Australia-wide targeting the educational, entertainment, and hobby needs of the home and small office market.

The identity projects personal service through the relaxed, fun figure of a person with a computer head. The symbol is very flexible, and adapts to promotional use and advertising.

Bed Shed

This major retail franchise company specializes in just about everything associated with beds and bedrooms.

The graphic of a "turned down bed" was used for architectural signage, point-of-purchase material, and all business stationery, and clearly differentiated the organization from its competitors while making a strong statement about the type of products they sell.

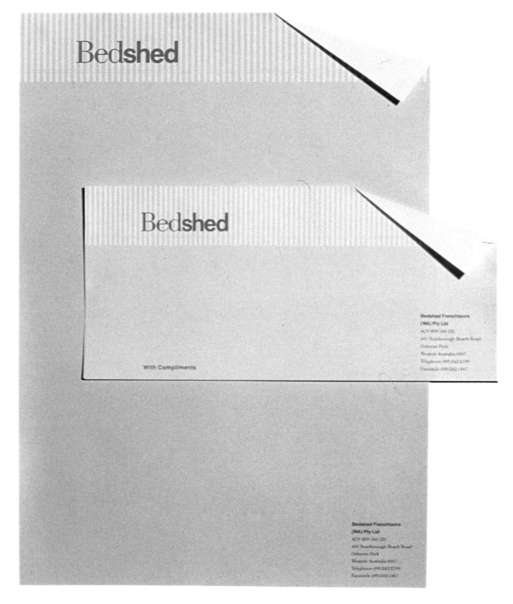

Nihon Sieber Hegner K.K.

A Japanese manufacturer of a wide range of industrial hearing products. After selecting the name Earfit, the accompanying graphics communicated the concept of "diminishing sound" by using varied weights of type.

National Dairies

Pura, the first national brand of milk, was launched by National Dairies in Australia. Bold, bright graphics instantly informed the consumer about the type of milk, and provided pertinent information on the front of the packs for this new family of milks.

Wander Australia

Packaging for Fortagen, a chocolate vitamin supplement drink.

Robert Timms

A leading marketer of international coffee blends in Australia, Robert Timms wished to be clearly positioned as purveyors of fine quality coffees. The nine gold packs were redesigned to take advantage of what was then a new packaging material for coffee. The visual inspiration came from the company's flagship blend from New Guinea, where the Bird of Paradise is the national symbol.

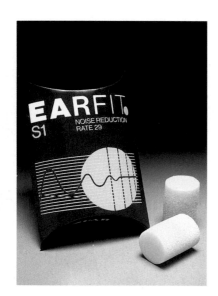

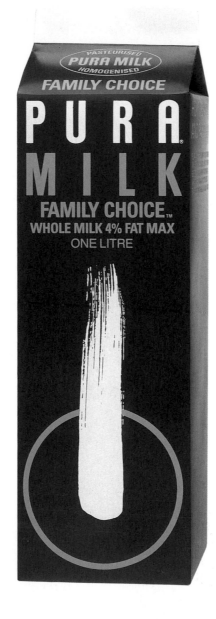

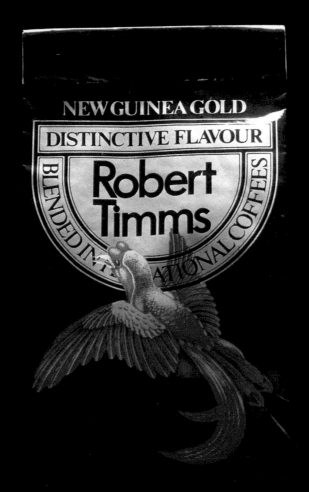

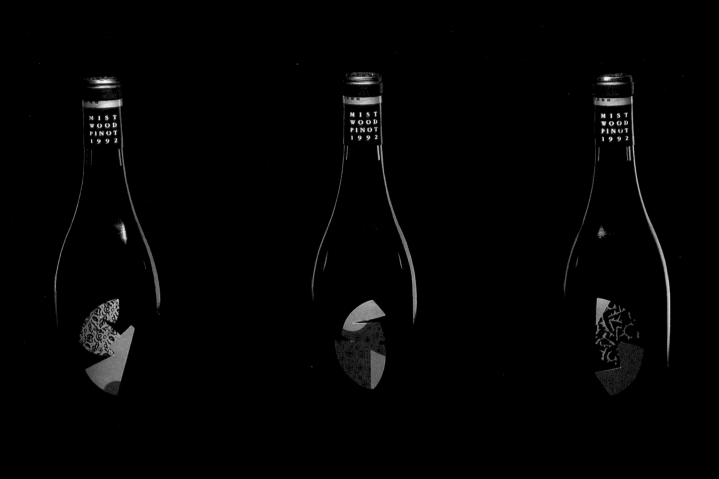

Mistwood

This small Victorian vineyard is also Cato's folly. The labels change each year to reflect the attributes of each vintage and the different varieties of wines produced in the vineyard. The Pinot Noir features twelve variations to the labels, making each bottle in a case different, while remaining part of the set.

A boutique winery in Victoria, Australia. Because of its size it faces enormous competition when it comes to marketing and merchandising wines. One of its most distinctive wines is Holystone, a blend of pinot noir and chardonnay. Cato chose a clear glass bottle to highlight the color of the wine.

The main label design, which has particular appeal for women, consists of a decoupage of old-fashioned roses and it is actually a double-sided label on the back of the bottle. The roses are magnified through the bottle, acting as a backdrop to the small branding label on the front.

The production of JV VI was a joint venture between six partners, hence the name and combined images forming a single portrait on the neck label.

Demi-vache was a dessert wine that was produced in limited quantities and only sold in half bottles. The graphics are as voluptuous as the wine.

The name T'Gallant has its origins in sea lore (it means "top sail".) The name was chosen because the winery is located near the ocean. The visual concept for the Pinot Grigio '94 was based on nautical flags.

Winemakers Kevin McCarthy and Kathleen Quealy have pioneered the development of Pinot Grigio in Australia. While the style of the wine is traditionally Italian, the design of the KKO1 label was anything but. The contrast worked. The entire vintage sold out in a month.

The "strip" diecut label for the T'Gallant 1993 Chardonnay created a sophisticated mystique designed to appeal to those who know their chardonnay, yet are still adventurous in their selection.

Celia's White Pinot is named after the winemakers' daughter. This barrel-aged white wine is positioned as an affordable "special occassion" wine. The style of the wine appeals to female consumers, a factor emphasized in the label design.

Heileman Brewing Company

This American company needed to upgrade its packaging on Lone Star, a Texan brand of beer. The hunting theme of the advertising communication was incorporated into the packaging, emphasizing the strong emotional link to the outdoors.

DB Breweries

A special promotional six-pack designed as gifts for the New Zealand company's staff and suppliers.

Tasmanian Breweries

The identity of Cascade Real Ale supported the traditional heritage of the dark, rich color and malt flavor of ale.
Cascade Premium Lager was launched to compete specifically with the premium and imported segment of the market. The label employed an illustration of the distinctive, but regrettably extinct, Tasmanian Tiger.

South Pacific Brewery

Papua New Guinea's largest producer of beer, South Pacific Brewery, has won a number of international beer competitions. To be successful in exporting to overseas markets, they required highly competitive packaging. The strategy was to create packaging that evoked a product positioning of the "beer from paradise".

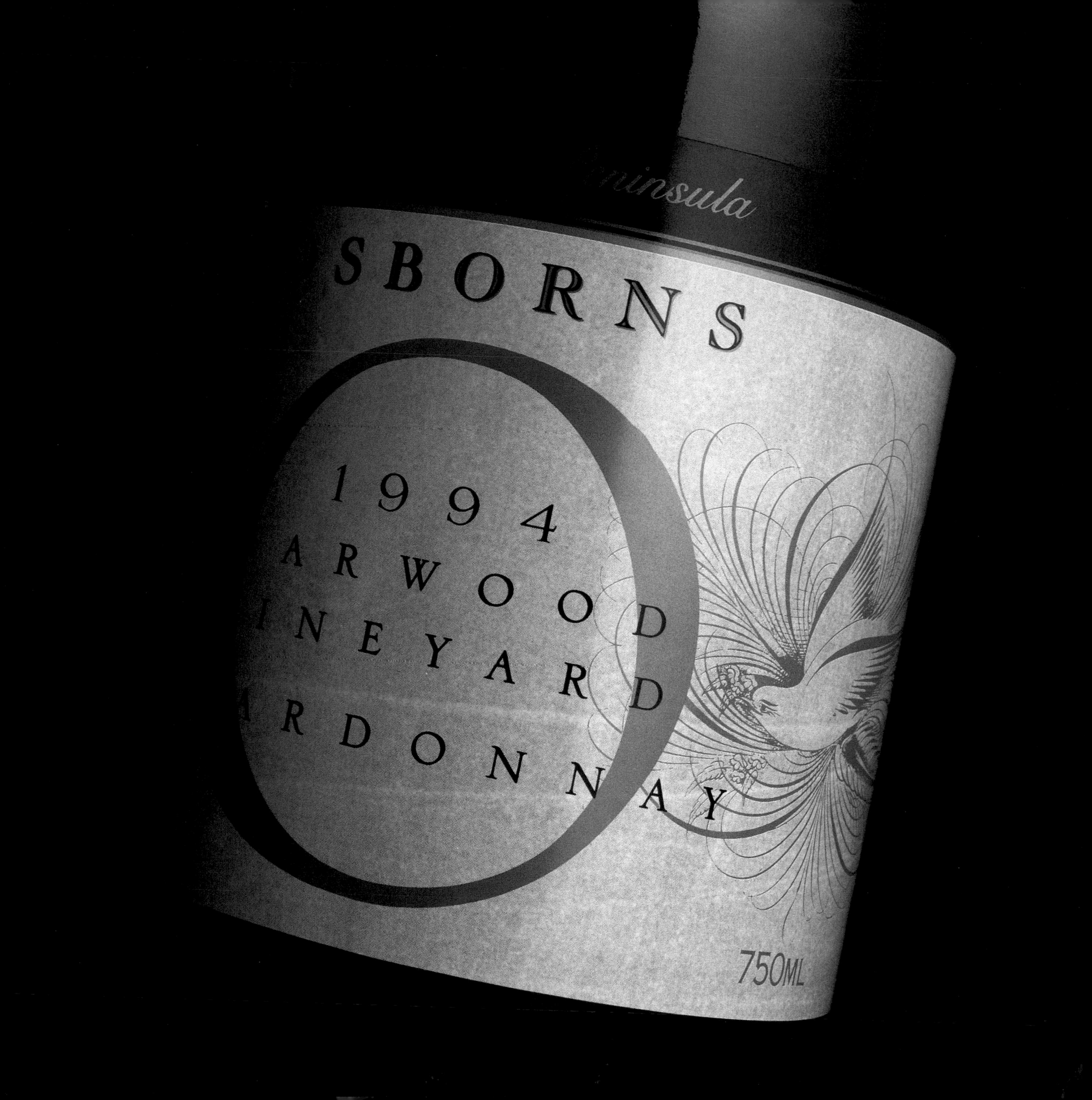
SBORNS
1994
ARWOOD
INEYARD
ARDONNAY
750ML

Harwood Vineyard

A small vineyard in Australia owned by the Osborn family. The series of labels depicted the exquisite birds which inhabit the area, and incorporated the "O" of Osborn as a brand mark on all product packaging.

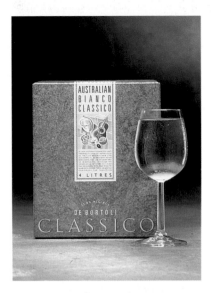

The original De Bortoli vineyards, established in Australia in 1928, were initially famous for their dessert wines. They have established further vineyards in the Yarra Valley district where they are producing Italian-style cask wines under the brand name of "Alfresco".

In order to add value to their range of quality products, and as part of a marketing strategy to present their products in sets, Tupperware decided to redesign their packaging.

Since the products never appear in a competitive retail environment, it was possible to remove the normally prerequisite descriptive copy from the packs, resulting in a series of gift-style boxes.

Product inserts were designed to complement the innovative packaging, incorporating important usage details, recipes, helpful tips, and cross-selling copy.

The top-of-the-line positioning of Tupperware products was conveyed throughout the product range from baby sets to barbecue products.

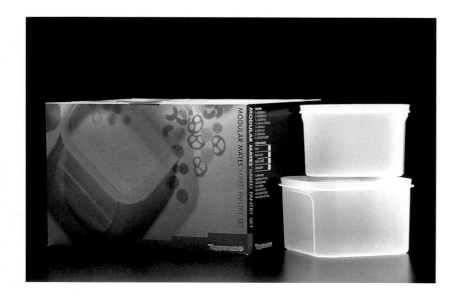

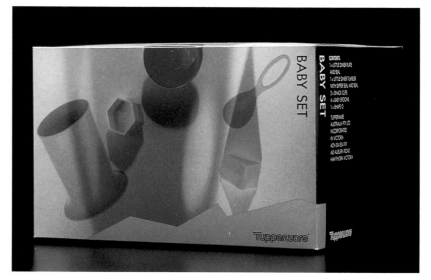

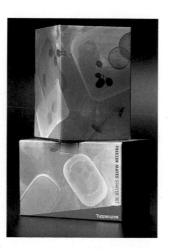

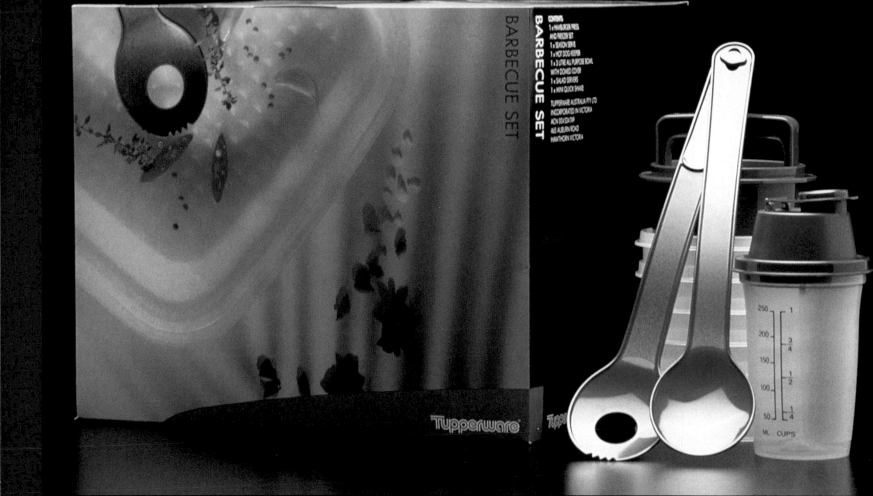

BARBECUE SET

BARBECUE SET

CONTAINS
1 x HAMBURGER PRESS
AND FREEZER SET
1 x SEASON SERVE
1 x HOT DOG KEEPER
1 x 3 LITRE ALL PURPOSE BOWL
WITH DOMED COVER
1 x SALAD SERVER
1 x MINI QUICK SHAKE

TUPPERWARE AUSTRALIA PTY LTD
INCORPORATED IN VICTORIA
ACN 004 934 769
465 AUBURN ROAD
HAWTHORN VICTORIA

250

200

150

100

50

ML   CUPS

Tupperware

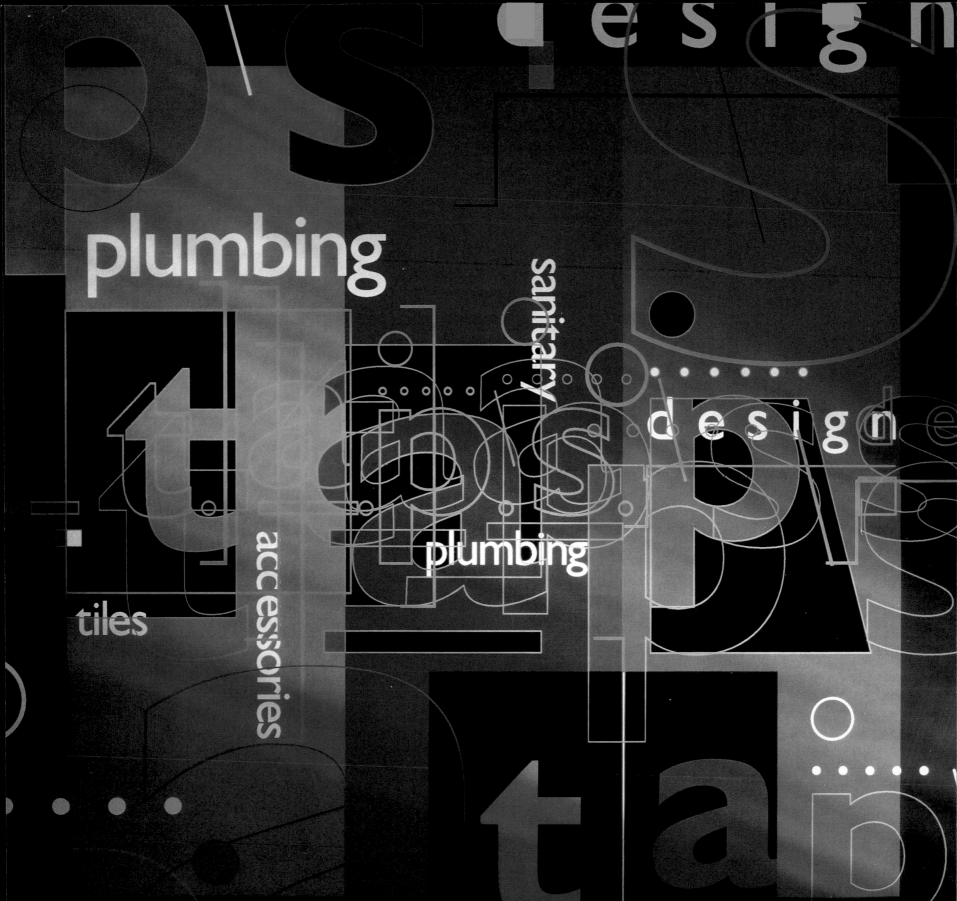

Rogers Seller & Myhill

T.A.P.S. DESIGN (Tiles, Accessory, Plumbing, Sanitary, are Australian importers of specialty "designer" hardware targeting the needs of architects, interior designers, and up-market building contractors. The identity projected a modern, highly graphic, and architectural feel that produced a suitable environment for the products in the showroom, and print materials and stationery.

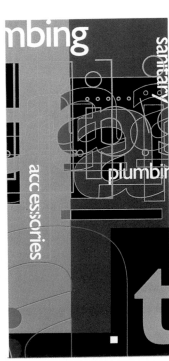

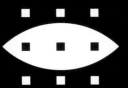

TS+B

BUXTON

Architectural graphics. Building on design *In the last ten years the rigid delineations of the different dimensions of design have become quietly and purposely blurred and overlapped. Architects, graphic designers, interior designers, and product designers now tend to combine their skills and offer synergistic approaches to design problems. This more holistic approach has the positive effect of creating more visually stimulating and relevant environments, while opening up new avenues for the designer. Design has a profound influence on how people relate to their environment and inevitably makes a statement far beyond simple expressions of function. There is the simple matter of a sign which can do far more than just provide direction. It can help position the venue or the organization, enhance the environment, create an ambience, and provide a multitude of information.*

Carringbush, property development, Australia.
Likas Square, building complex, Malaysia.
Laminex Industries, manufacturer of building products, Australia.

Sankyo Aluminium, Japan.
Trollope, Silverwood & Beck, manufacturers and shopfitters, Australia.
Buxton Consolidated, property development, Australia.

Queensland Marble, Australia.
Likas View, construction company, Malaysia.
Landplan, property development, New Zealand.

Landcorp An integrated identity for the harbour city of Bunbury, Australia, incorporating directional signage, corporate stationery, and promotional material.

One of the oldest architectural firms in Australia specializing in design and documentation of high quality retail architecture including shopping centers, large recreational and sporting complexes, and industrial and commercial projects.

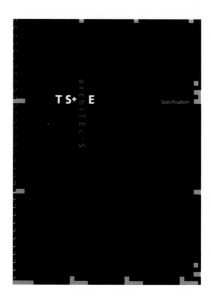

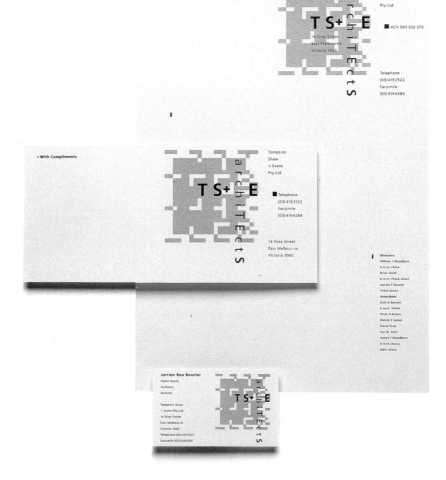

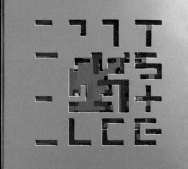
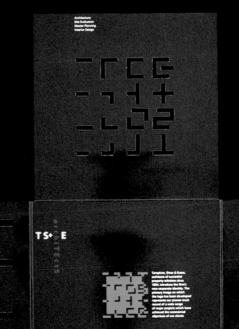

Laminex Industries

The exhibition was created to display
a major new product and color range.
Innovative, over-size invitational
posters using a variety of three-
dimensional forms created interest
and a sense of anticipation.

The exhibition illustrated the diverse range of uses and applications of the products. Through the use of 20, three-dimensional sculptures, over 60 finishes were highlighted.

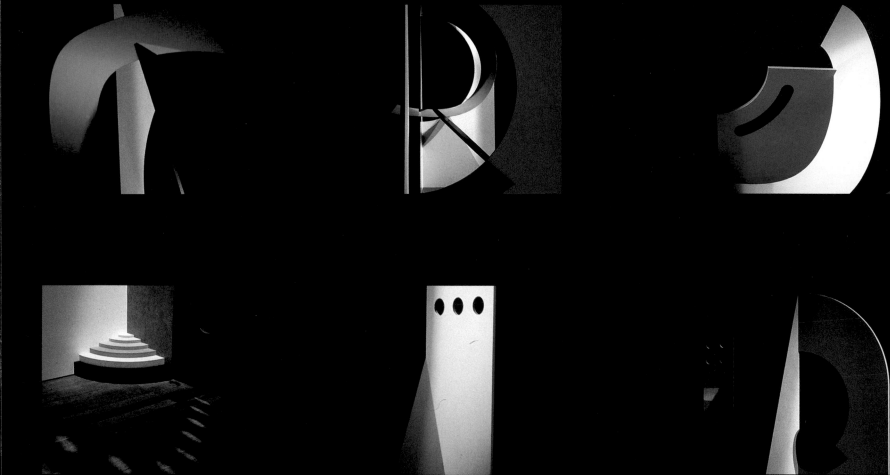

Pidemco Land

A major Singaporean property development and investment company. To emphasize their core business, the identity incorporated the use of an isometric drawing of the city grid, which adapted the graphic elements to its vertical and horizontal planes.

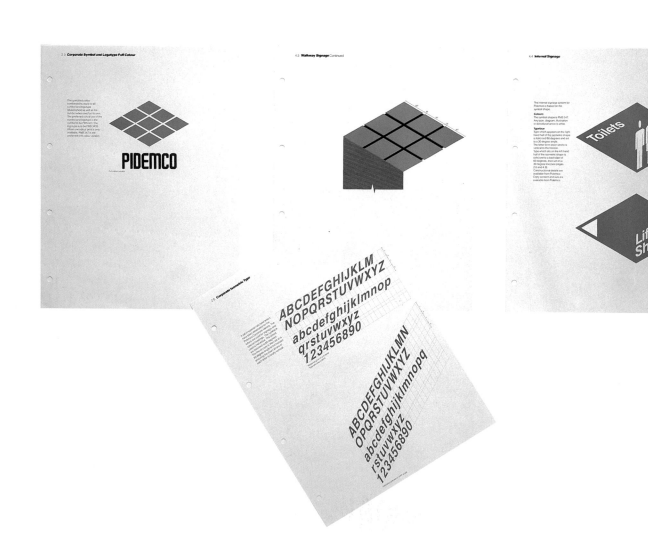

East Perth Redevelopment Authority

The largest and most exciting urban renewal project ever undertaken in Western Australia. This previously industrial land was transformed into an urban community on the shore of the Swan River.

One of the most significant aims of the project was environmental sensitivity while using Perth's natural geography to its best advantage.

The identity developed was based on the black swan, the symbol of Western Australia. Architectural projections and lines brought visual balance between a man-made development and nature.

Site markers and sign boards adapted the symbol in different three-dimensional forms.

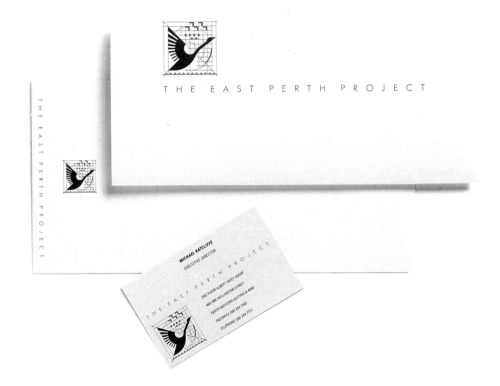

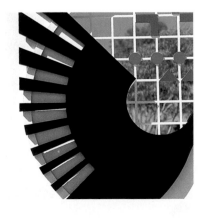

C'est La Vie Corporation

A privately owned land development company based in Japan, known for the design and construction of luxury homes in Ashiya, a residential area outside Osaka.

The corporate identity evolved from C'est La Vie's corporate philosophy that man should live in harmony with his built and natural environments.

The identity, based on the simplest architectural form, allowed enormous flexibility to incorporate individual projects while maintaining a strong sense of the main identity. The square was reconstructed to extend its boundaries, providing distinct identities for each architectural project.

The square was then extended to use the seven geometric shapes of the tangram, a square Chinese puzzle. These formed human figures which reflected the ultimate users of the buildings. The tangram pieces allowed infinite possibilities.

C'est La Vision, the creation of a total retail concept for the C'est La Vie Corporation, including the development of the main identity, and a number of branded product lines to be sold in the exclusive retail outlets.

Extensions of C'est La Vision's "eye" graphic and the variations of the tangram were used as motifs on a variety of products including stationery, clothing, leather goods, and packaging.

Eco, an environmentally sensitive brand created for C'est La Vision, uses the shapes of the tangram to form abstract trees made of human forms, and represents the evolution of other animal and bird shapes.

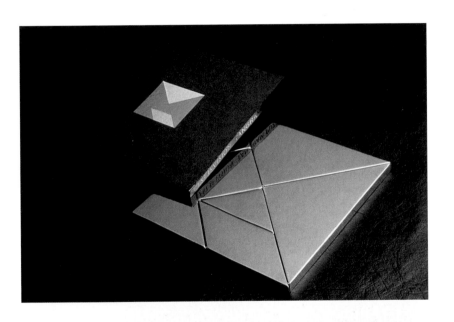

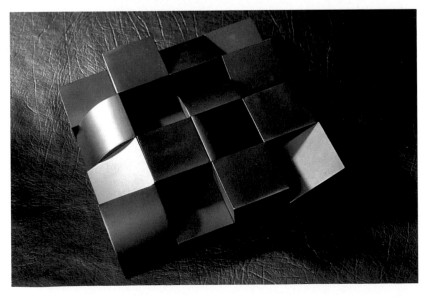

Limited Editions

Limited Editions, a distinctive range
of gift items designed by Cato including
cutlery, ceramics, place card holders,
and executive puzzles.

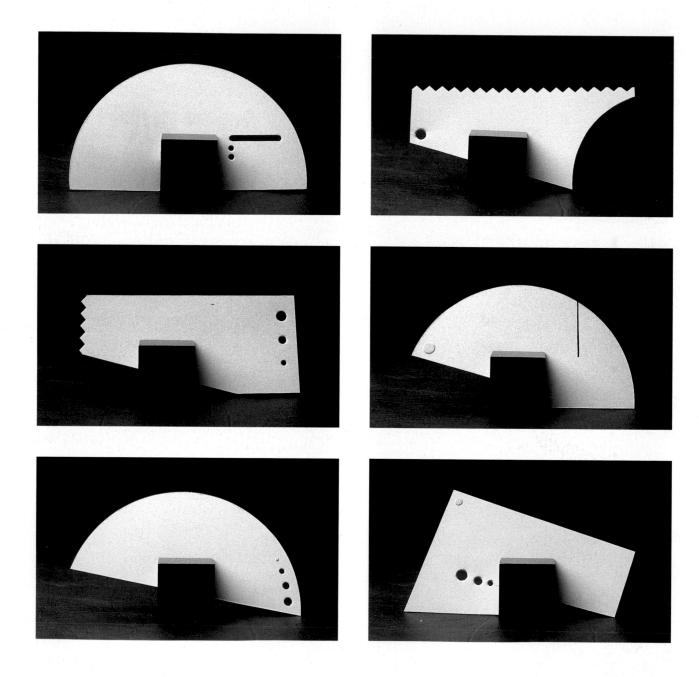

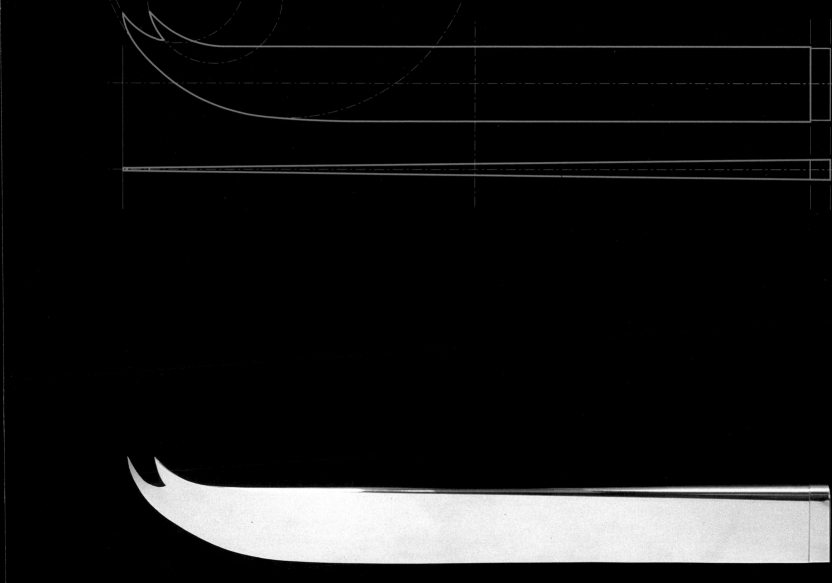

Annual Guest Card
The Qantas Club
This card admits one guest in the company of the member
The Qantas Club
Membership
Member since
Valid until end

Transport: Going places with design *In most cases, the visual identity of any major transport system will affect millions of people every day. Airlines rarely have any real point of difference besides their livery. The planes are basically the same size and configuration, the cabin crew serve similar meals and offer the same sort of amenities, and the seats recline according to the class of the ticket purchased. Design solutions for transport depend on clarity of communication. Often the ultimate inspiration does not depend on complete originality but on the perception of information in a new and different way.*

Qantas Airways

The image of a kangaroo with her joey formed the background for the Qantas Club visual identity.

This reinterpretation of the main Qantas symbol, the kangaroo, reinforces the airline's most memorable image and connects the lounge program with its source.

The new identity brought together the Flight Deck and Captain's Club lounges worldwide.

The luggage tags utilize patterns from aerial photographic images of the different landscapes of Australia.

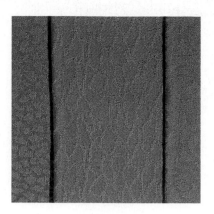

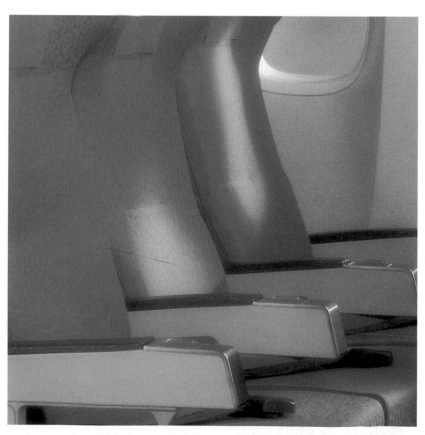

À LA CARTE MENU

WINE LIST

MENU AND BAR LIST

MENU

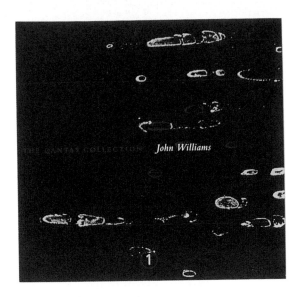

John Williams

To emphasize the customer service image of the new Qantas, the Annual Report 1993–94 focused on the people that make it one of the world's leading airlines. Interior and exterior photography captured Qantas employees continuing the tradition of excellence that Qantas has always upheld. New covers and formats for the Entertainment Guides, and gifts of CDs for First Class Passengers, all add to Qantas' commitment to its customers.

Australian Chamber Orchestra

1 **Mozart** Symphony No. 29 in A Major, K. 201
4th Movement 'Allegro con spirito'
2 **Barber** Adagio for Strings, Op. 11a
3 **Elgar** Serenade for Strings, Op. 20 1st Movement 'Allegro piacevole'
4 **Mendelssohn** Sinfonia No. 9 in C, 'Swiss' 2nd Movement 'Andante'

5 **J.S. Bach** Orchestral Suite No. 3 in D Major, BWV1068 1st Movement 'Overture'
6 **Janacek** Kreutzer Sonata for Strings
3rd Movement 'Con moto (Vivace–Andante)'
7 **Mozart** Adagio in E for violin and orchestra, K. 261
8 **Grieg** Holberg Suite, Op. 40
2nd Movement 'Sarabande – Andante'
9 **Mozart** Rondo in C
for violin and orchestra, K. 373

Qantas Annual Report 1993–94

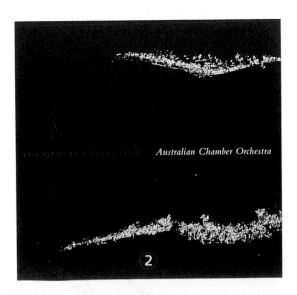

Australian Chamber Orchestra

ROTT
NEST
LODGE

Hospitality. Feeling at home with design *Design is an integral part of the positioning of any hotel. Often the attributes of the hotel are reflected in its collateral material. They may be only small but they are important tangible differences that benefit from good design.*
The hospitality industry has been one of the biggest growth areas worldwide. Most hotel groups have realized the importance of the hotel environment as an oasis for their weary guests. The large international hotel chains offer a familiar ambience in many countries. The furnishings, menus, and artefacts provide a home away from home. Many hotels create a variety of environments within the main environment offering exotic and international food and beverage outlets. Design is the one element that remains with the guest throughout their stay. The effect of design will influence the guest long before they arrive, and be a strong determining factor together with location, facilities, and service in the decision to make a return visit.

Burswood Resort Hotel, Australia.
Park Royal Hotel, Brisbane, Australia.
NTT Prio Health Club, Japan.

Rottnest Lodge.
Reflecting the resort's history, atmosphere, and location, the identity adapted easily to interior design and marketing needs.

Palm Meadows Resort and Golf Club, Australia.
Breakers Restaurant, Mirage Resort Hotel, Australia.
Golf Resorts International, Australia.

Grand Hyatt Jakarta.
Restaurant identities reflecting local culture, and western and Asian cues that also contribute to the international feel of the hotel.

Raffles Hotel

The historic Raffles Hotel had been languishing under the bright lights of modern Singapore. After a two-year restoration period, Raffles Hotel is once again the epitome of the lavish colonial style.

A combination of period styles, cultural cues, and authentic techniques were incorporated in the formal Victorian motifs in the Raffles Grill, Writers Bar, Empire Cafe, and the more eclectic East meets West designs of Ah Teng's Bakery.

Dusit Inn Balikpapan

The identity of this four star resort included signage, guest room compendium, stationery, shopping bags, and individual identities for the mix of international food and beverage outlets.

Citraland Hotel Jakarta

Integrated identity for the hotel and a variety of hotel facilities, and food and beverage outlets.

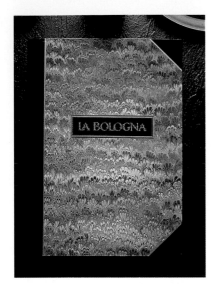

Marina Mandarin Hotel

The identity of this Singapore hotel reflected its stunning waterside location. The initials, represented in a highly stylized oriental motif that alluded to the reflection of water, made up the elements of the symbol for this luxury hotel.

Also created were individual identities for the different food and beverage outlets in the hotel.

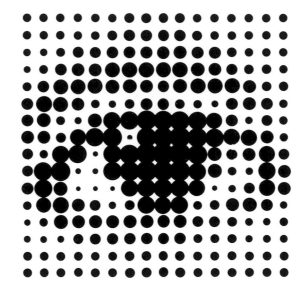

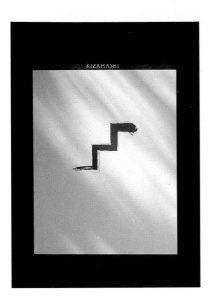

Hyatt Regency Surabaya

This Indonesian hotel was conceived as "a wealthy western mansion" that displayed national artifacts.

It was important for the interior of the hotel to project an ambience that was welcoming to both the international traveller and the local residents. The main identity is reflected in all print material and signage.

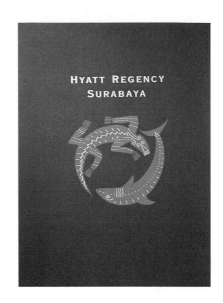

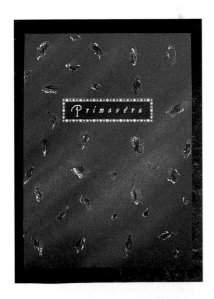

Hyatt Regency Johor Bahru
The identity for one of the leading international business hotels in Johor Bahru, Malaysia, extended to the food and beverage outlets, guest room stationery, and amenities and signage program.

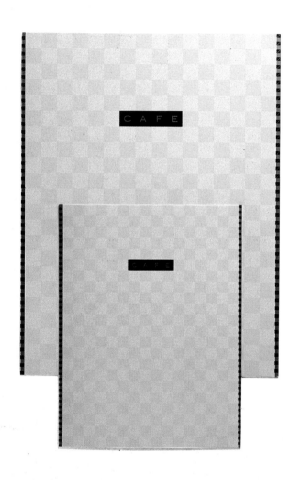

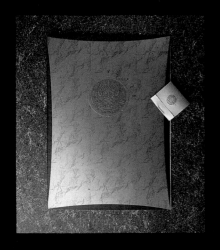

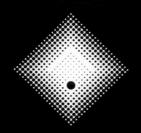

Institutional identities. Making a mark *The ultimate success of an institution depends on its ability to be seen as credible, effective, and worthy of funding. Projecting an appropriate identity can play a crucial role in communicating these strategic points. A strong identity can shift the perceptions and attitudes of those employed in or using the institution; it can motivate potential sponsors and influence the press to speak highly of the organization.*

The Australian Centre for American Studies, Australia.
National Skin Centre, specialist dermatological clinic, Singapore.
Department of Productivity, government department, Australia.

Victoria University of Technology, Australia.
Alzheimer Society of Victoria, Australia.
Toa Payoh Hospital, Singapore.

Department of Youth, Sport and Recreation, government department, Australia.
Snowy Mountains Hydro Electric Scheme, Australia.
2nd New Zealand Crafts Biennale.

Museum of Victoria Annual Report. The concept was based on a collage of museum icons including masks, skulls, indigenous people, and extinct animals forming a portrait of a human head.

John Truscott Foundation

John Truscott was the driving force behind the Melbourne International Festival of the Arts, the Victorian Arts Centre, and World Expo '88.

After his death a trust was set up to offer support to young Australian artists.

Truscott's flamboyant signature was the basis for the identity and was interpreted in painting and sculpture.

The element of the design is flexible so each project can have its own identity while being recognized as part of the foundation.

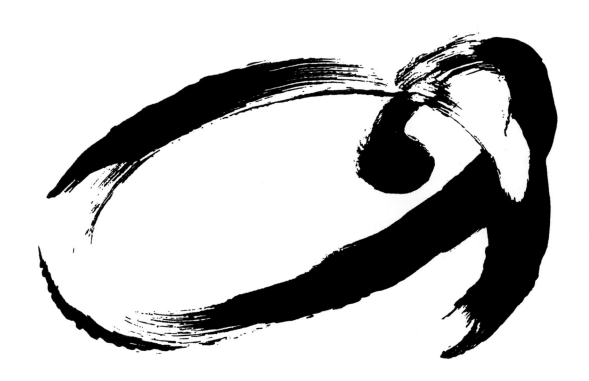

MFP Australia

A multi-function polis integrating urban and community development. It is a project about the interaction between people and technology, and seeks international cooperation in developing a city of the future.

It encompasses, among other facilities, an international center for research and education, and a center for international business investment in new and emerging technologies. A number of strong, visual components were linked together to support the main symbol which effectively communicated an understanding of the project's dimensions.

State Library of Victoria

The State Library of Victoria is housed in a marvellous Victorian building in Melbourne, Australia. The identity and signage program clearly positioned the library, and reflected its heritage. The concept for the identity was based on an open book format which was interpreted in metal for the signage as an effective way to guide visitors through the library's facilities.

The signage system allowed the flexible use of scale to harmonize with different proportions in the various building spaces. The signs were able to carry extensive information, and the concept worked well for temporary exhibitions.

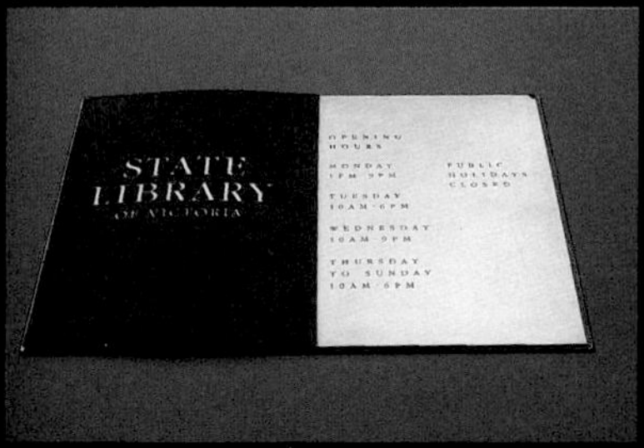
STATE
LIBRARY
OF VICTORIA
OPENING HOURS
PUBLIC HOLIDAYS CLOSED
TUESDAY
WEDNESDAY
THURSDAY TO SUNDAY

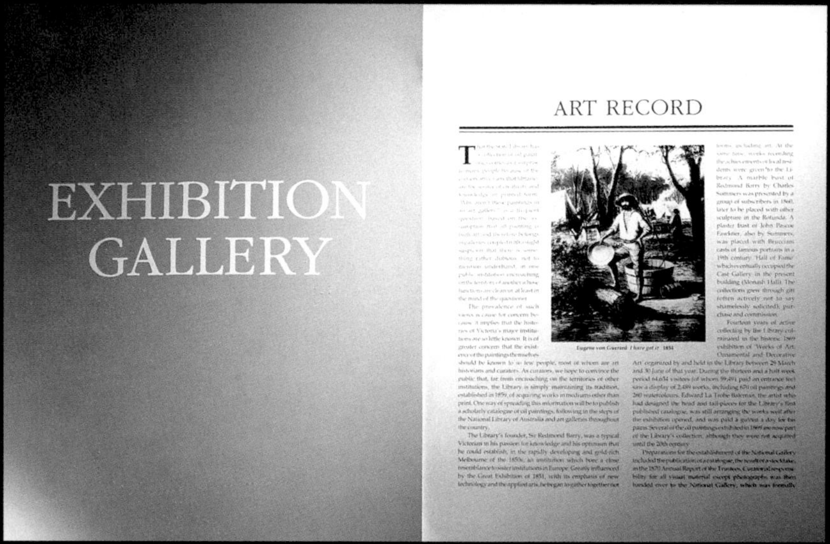
EXHIBITION
GALLERY
ART RECORD

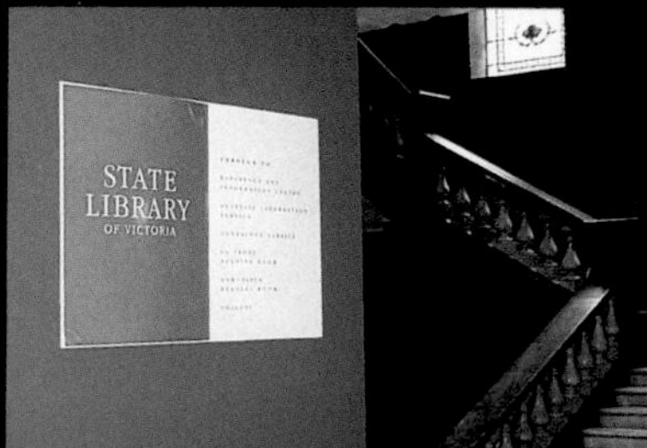
STATE
LIBRARY
OF VICTORIA

ΛЯC

The corporate visual language *A company's presence and tone of voice pervade all its activity; communications are the core of business. To articulate the identity a visual strategy must be employed. The main role of the designer is to help ensure the corporate identities have integrity and compelling visual cues. In today's global business environment a strong visual identity is one of the most important marketing and communications tools a company can have. It is therefore crucial that it is carefully developed and nurtured, so each communication builds a clear, focused identity that their audiences can easily and correctly interpret. Design has a very simple function. It communicates. Quite simply, the visual message crosses the cultural boundaries and is the easiest to understand.*

Beautyware, manufacturers of bathroom products, Australia.
BWN Sliding Door Company, manufacturers of "Live Oil" a process for cleaning.
Addit Australia, computer products.

Applied Research Corporation, government funded research company, Singapore.
Miles Kyowa, industrial chemical company, Japan.
Mimi Japan / Australia, gas exploration.

Austral Pacific Corporation, business investment and holding company, New Zealand.
Mycal Bears, grid iron football team, Japan.
Australian Medical Enterprises, healthcare.

Creative Infomatics.
Symbol for an Australian training company representing the close working relationship between their clients and themselves.

BHP Petroleum

A subsidiary of Australia's largest and best known company, BHP, sought a dramatic and relevant signage program for their headquarters. Ideally, it needed to link the architecture with the main function of the company, oil and gas exploration.

The inspiration came from the seismic profile of the first location where BHP discovered oil, and utilized some of the metals produced by the company.

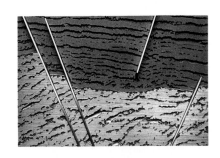

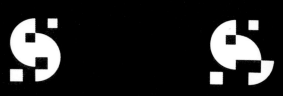

Sealcorp Holdings

Sealcorp is the parent and strategic base for four well-known financial and investment advisory companies: Asgard, Assirt, Securitor, and Pact.

The visual resolution of the identity was based on the graphic interpretation of financial pie-charts. The concept was then systematically adapted to a family of integrated symbols applied throughout the organization's print and signage program.

Lend Lease Corporation

A major Australian property services company which has expanded and diversified its many business interests dramatically since the company started in 1986.

The identity needed to clearly show that the divisions including insurance, construction, and finance, all belonged to the one parent company, while reflecting the independent management approach of each division.

Kern Corporation

Collins Street in Melbourne, Australia, is one of the most prestigious addresses in the central business district.

When Kern Corporation, one of Australia's largest land development corporations, decided to redevelop 101 Collins Street, they required an identity that reflected the distinguished positioning of the building.

Mallesons Stephen Jaques

A large, prestigious international law firm based in Australia, with offices in London and New York, and major cities throughout South East Asia, required a corporate identity that reflected their history, mission, and strategic direction.

The identity needed to be adapted for legal documents, all stationery, tender documents, marketing material, and electronic mail and media items.

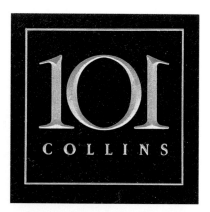

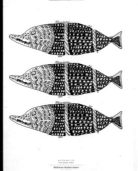

Mallesons Stephen Jaques

Mallesons Stephen Jaques

Mallesons Stephen Jaques

Mallesons Stephen Jaques

Mallesons Stephen Jaques

PRINZ
PRINZ
PRINZ

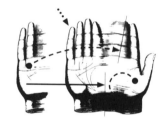

Judging by appearances *Talking to those who are visually aware is often the designer's most demanding task. It is not only about communications but also the judgments based on the quality of aesthetics. The effective usage of a broader visual language can be clearly seen in the work done by those in graphic-related professions. Designers respond strongly to corporations whose material*

stimulates the senses. Traditionally print material is seen as the format for design, but technology and televisual communications are evidence of the increase in design-conscious communication. We all judge by appearances. The power of what the designers provide is understood by very few corporations. Those that utilize the power of design are known to us all.

Institute of Public Relations, Singapore.
Public Relations Institute of
New Zealand.
Sorrett, publishing company, Australia.

Full Stop, typesetting house, Australia.
The Right Hand Corporate
Communications, Australia.
Australian Audio Visual.

Hedgehog, public relations company,
Australia.
Imagistics, audio visual house,
Australia.
The Name Register, naming company,
Australia.

Observatoire Internationale des Priso
non-profit poster.
Advertising Print Production
Association, poster promoting Cato a
guest speaker.

GARD NER
CULTIVATING THE CRAFT OF LITHOGRAPHY

GARD NER
CULTIVATING THE CRAFT OF LITHOGRAPHY

WITH COMPLIMENTS

GARDNER PRINTING CO (VIC) PTY LTD 36 THORNTON CRESCENT MITCHAM TELEPHONE (03) 874 2131
ALL CORRESPONDENCE TO BE ADDRESSED TO PO BOX 175 NUNAWADING VICTORIA AUSTRALIA 3131

Gardner Press

This visual identity program was for a well-established printery, Gardner Press. Their name provided an opportunity to add greater meaning to the word.

Utilizing visual cues related to "gardeners", then using those symbols on the letterhead and related stationery items, the identity graphically demonstrated what the company did and how well they did it.

Vega Press

Vega Press started out as a small but aggressive print house with a commitment to quality color printing. To reflect their positioning as specialists, design was used to create an identity which demonstrated the quality of their four-color printing.

A series of high-impact, three-dimensional mailing pieces were also developed including the "Blackbirds" calendar.

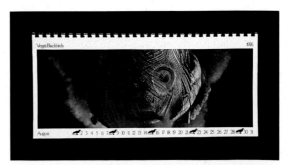

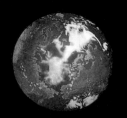
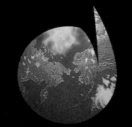
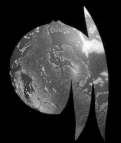

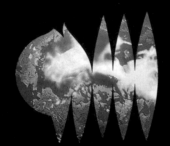

SBS Television

A multicultural television station in Australia, broadcasting programs from all over the world. The station identification and promotions used the graphics of the globe, representing their commitment to multicultural programming.

The predominant color for the identity was blue, from the earth as seen from outer space. Cartographic treatment of the globe gives meaning and distinction to the symbol. The unravelling segments lie flat, enabling the earth's entire surface to be seen.

Five of these segments, representing the five continents, were then tilted on an angle from the earth's axis of 22.5 degrees.

Its distinct and numerous possibilities of form provided great opportunities on-screen and it has been successfully integrated into the print media.

136 **Cato Design Inc**

Edge *is an internationally distributed*
magazine which informs current clients
of changes in the Asia Pacific Basin in
terms of attitudes and influences on
design, and keeps them up-to-date on
the company's work in the region.
Each issue uses a variety of different
papers and techniques.

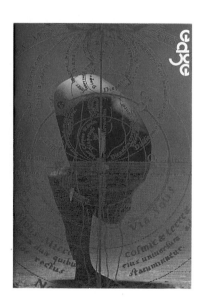

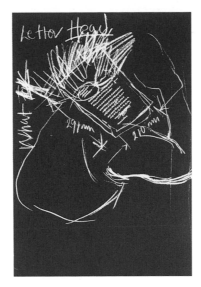

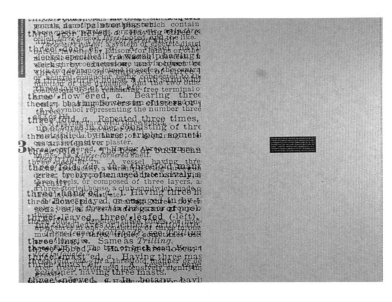

A^4

Portmans

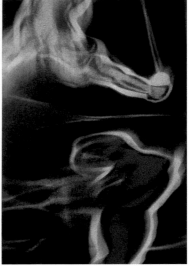

SHE
SHOWS
ITS
SU
PPORT

Y

rich

ROBERT WILK IN JAPAN NEW RICH

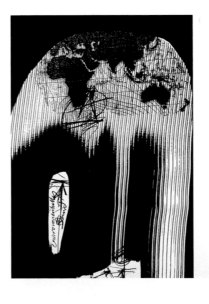

Urbane Publicity

A Japanese studio specializing in high quality, still life, commercial photography commissioned a folio that would appeal internationally.

The solution came in a specially constructed perforated metal container, designed to hold a set of limited edition prints.

This intriguing presentation provided a distorted view of the photographs within, focusing on the concept that photographs "happen" first as images of color, shape, and composition in the mind, with no finality and detail until executed.

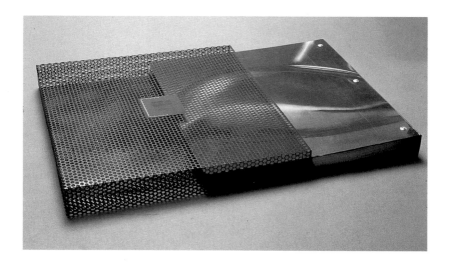

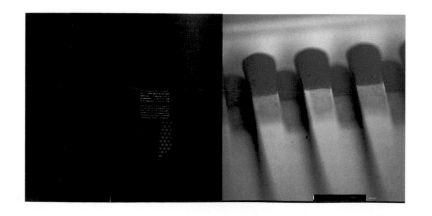

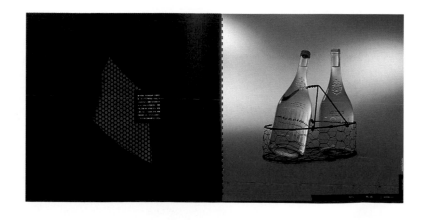

Printflo Marketing

The Singaporean division of Price & Pierce, one of the world's largest paper companies, Printflo purchases print material from different suppliers throughout Asia.

The company required a separate identity from the parent company.

In creating a highly individual look, a variety of typefaces were reproduced in different colors and a number of embellishments were used to demonstrate the variety of printing techniques they could offer.

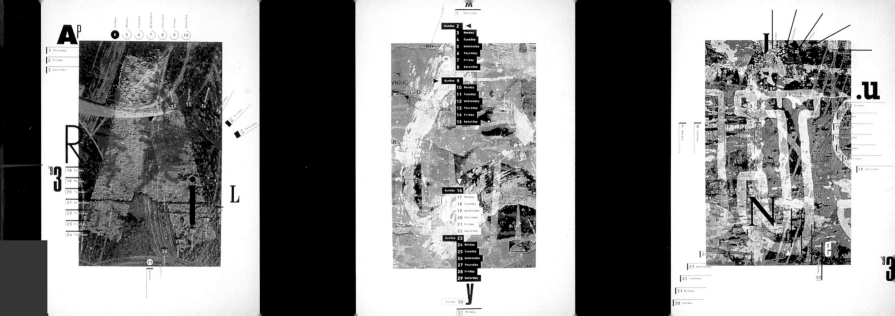

Murder records spread to more U.S. cities, suburbs

By Tom Squitieri
USA TODAY

The USA rings in the New Year with what's becoming an annual tradition: the setting of record murder ra...

With two days left in the bloodiest year ever, at least 23 big cities beat records — for the third straight year.

Eight other major cities are on the verge of joining the list.

Tracking a surge in murders that began in 1989, the total murder estimate for 1991 is 23,700 — up 300 from 1990.

Experts see no leveling off, unp...

"This is not a problem in one neighborhood or one segment of the city. It's the whole city," says police chief Bill Rathburn...

USA TODAY's survey shows:

▶ Medium-size cities once thought immune from the murderous terror of the Gothams are ...

▶ ...spreading into suburbs. One example: 6 of 7 Washington, D.C., suburbs set records this year; the seventh is one body away.

Disputes among friends or ... in a top cause, followed by the drug trade or rising gang activity ... influenced by easy access to firearms historically used in ... of ... murder ...

Experts agree that drug violence has cheapened life.

"... have to work a little harder to convince people ... life is worth living," says Police Chief Johnnie Johnson of Birmingham, Ala. which also set a record.

▶ Tracking murder, 3A

Internacional Del Cartel en Mexico

The poster portrayed "America Today 500 Years Later" as part of an exhibition at the Second International Biennial of the Poster in Mexico, 1992, which commemorated the five hundredth anniversary of the arrival of Christopher Columbus in the Americas.

Brotherhood of St Laurence

Poster to encourage those out of work and in distress to seek practical and positive aid at the Employment Action Centre set up by the charity of the Brotherhood of St Laurence.

The "Year of the Dog" diary is based on the Chinese lunar calendar. This collaboration with Shiro Pacific Paper uses a mixture of canine, free-form graphics, and eclectic images to form a highly sophisticated promotion piece.

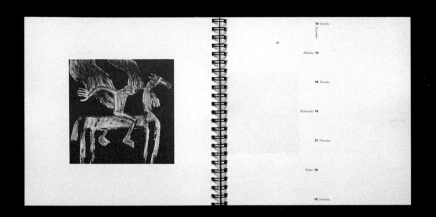

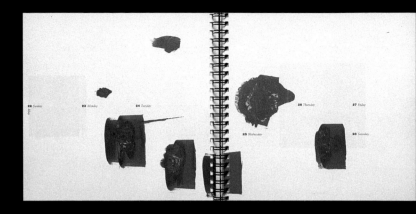

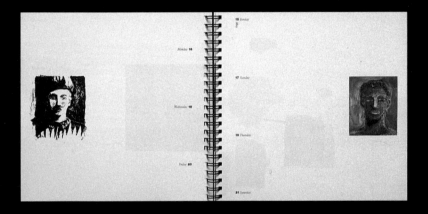

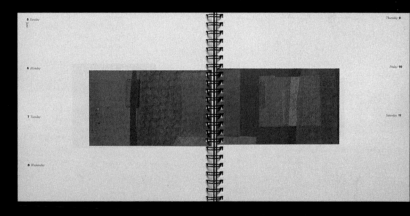

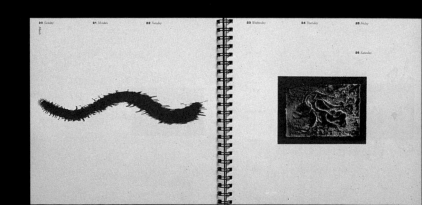

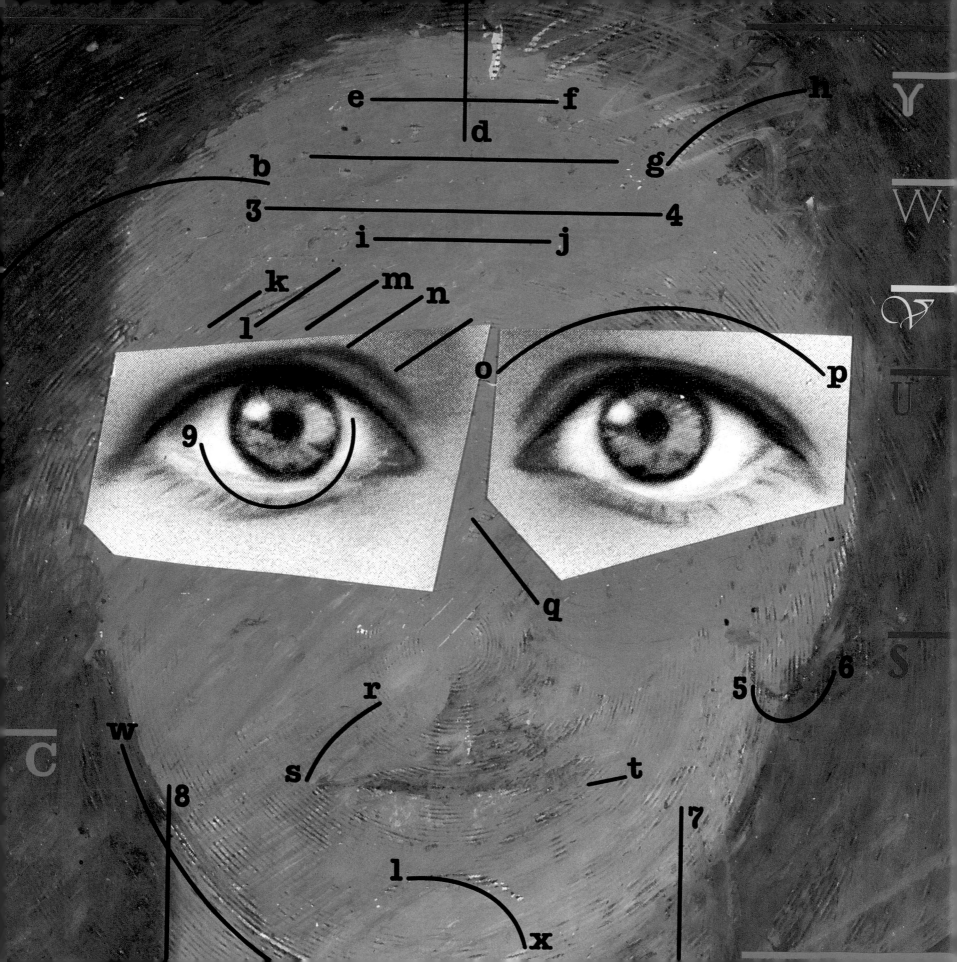

Epitype Australia

This typesetting company opened its doors aware that it was entering an already crowded market.

The design task was to develop a visual identity that distinguished Epitype from established competition and created an instant presence.

The logotype and a series of self-explanatory and eye-catching posters covered the different aspects of Epitype's activities.

Each poster provided information about type designers or demonstrated the typefaces available from the company.

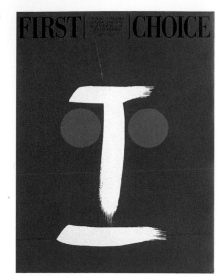

First Choice

Recognizing the challenge of selecting one's own favorite pieces of work, Cato conceived the idea of asking leading international designers for their personal choice. One hundred and thirty designers from all over the world contributed their work. The cover and internal graphic approach depict a stylized face and the number one, reflecting the highly personal nature of the book. Published in English and Japanese by Graphic-Sha, Japan.

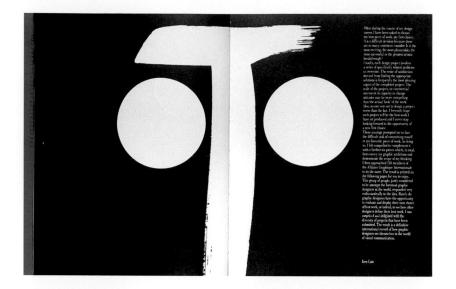

View from Australia

The first collective view of the skills and original ideas of Australia's leading graphic designers. More than 30 designers were represented in hundreds of projects demonstrating the development of Australian design and creating a valuable international reference. Published in English and Japanese by Graphic-Sha, Japan.

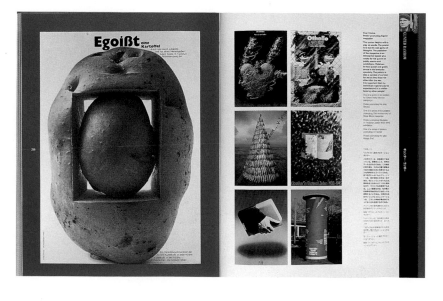

シカゴのヒッコリー・ビジネス・
ファニチャー のショールーム。
アメリカ・カリフォルニアでの
バンダービル・デザインの作品。

Showroom for Hickory
Business Furniture in
Chicago, by Vanderbyl
Design, California, 1958.

GD3D

Cato has long been interested in the developing role of graphic design in the built environment. The book is a collection of three-dimensional works from a wide selection of internationally renowned graphic designers. Published in English, German, and Japanese by Graphic-Sha in Japan.

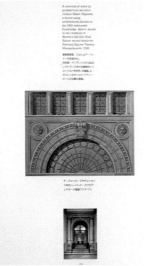

A selection of work by
architectural muralist
Joshua Winer. Opposite:
a mural using
architectural illusion in
the D&B restaurant,
Cambridge, Massachusetts.
Below: mural facade for
Harvard Square Theatre,
Massachusetts, 1988.

建物の壁面に、ジョシュア・ワイ
ナーの壁画が描かれている。

右：アメリカ・マサチューセッ
ツのハーバード・スクエア・シア
ターの壁面ファサード。

Beverly Reiser works
with light and colour
using neon, conditional
glass and various light
phenomena. Her
compositions are studies
in implied movement
featuring areas of
changing light and colour.

Ribbons in Love' for
Home Protection Hair
Salon in glass and neon
by Beverly Reiser, USA.

ベバリー・ライザーはネオン、
特殊加工ガラス、その他さまざま
な光の現象を利用している。光と色
彩の変化をとらえ、動きを暗示した
"動きの空間"を表現。

アメリカのHOメント・プロテク
ションのヘアサロン用の、ガラスと
ネオンによる"愛のリボン"。

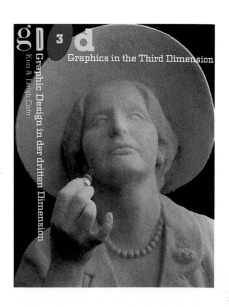

g·o 3 d
Graphic Design in der dritten Dimension
Graphics in the Third Dimension
Kent & Leigh Cato

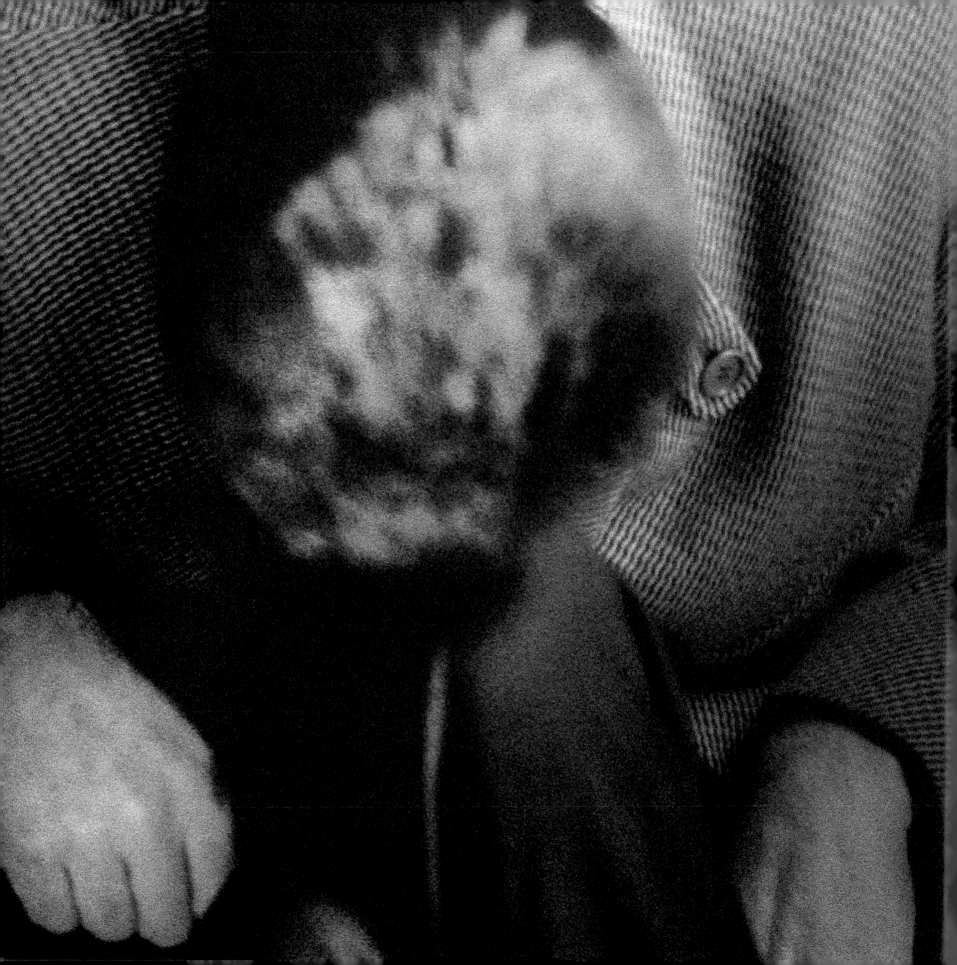

Work in Progress *"Our first 25 years have seen a lot of progress. The next 25 years will see us well into the twenty-first century. I believe that design will become a more recognized ingredient in successful business management. Already many governments in Asia are actively supporting the development of design. Our aim is to develop the company's resource network in the Pacific Basin, to offer our clients a complete range of services that can integrate all their visual communications needs. The role of design is expanding as its diversity is being recognized. Design is an exciting profession. Each project is different, requiring a variety of skills. It is never boring or routine. Every day we are faced with a series of great opportunities disguised as insolvable problems."* Ken Cato

Ken Cato is a member of the American Institute of Graphic Art, Alliance Graphique Internationale, ICOGRADA, Type Directors Club New York, Australian Writers and Art Directors Association, Australian Type Directors Club, Industrial Design Council of Australia, The Australian Academy of Design, and the Young Presidents' Organization. He is an Honorary Fellow of both the Design Institute of Australia, and the Australian Marketing Institute, and a Board Member of the Australian Centre for American Studies, as well as having been invited to be the first international honorary member of the Russian Academy of Graphic Design.

Cato projects.

New areas of exploration are always exhilarating, and further stretch talent and creativity. With this in mind Cato has developed a range of products and is pursuing opportunities with Asian manufacturers. The products reflect his own philosophy of living.

As he sees it, "We all judge by appearances, as well as just function, and although we make purchase decisions on performance, there is also a special pride and enjoyment in owning something that is beautiful in its own right. I very much believe that everything one sees, touches, tastes, and smells should enhance a state of being and feed the generosity of spirit.

The effect on the senses is the essence of style, and style is something everyone can possess. Style is not fashion, it is a comfort level, a fundamental understanding that experience is not just something that happens to you, but what you do with what happens to you.

Style is a simple way of reflecting our individual complexities. The effective design of furniture, homewares, apparel, and personal care products depends on the balance between the simplicity of line, the subtlety of pattern, the nuance of texture, the moods of hue, and in some cases the haunting aromas of scent."

KEN**C**ATO

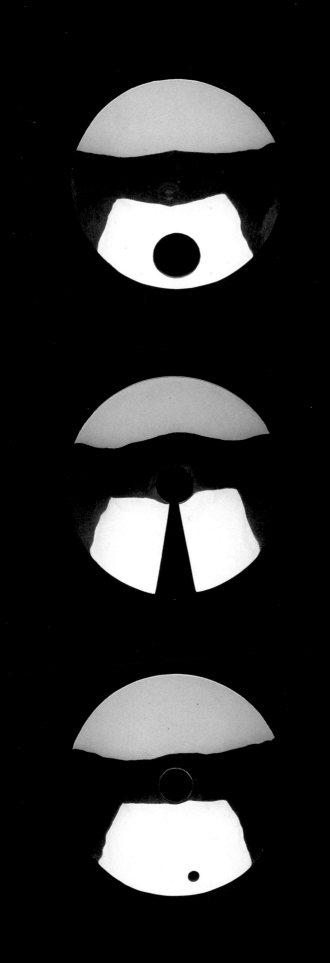

This selection from a book of handbags designed by Cato, which emphasizes the cut, classic geometric shapes, and quality look of 10 handbags, highlights accessories that are designed to be opulent in feel yet deceptively simple. Eco products are the essence of simplicity. These products are aesthetic and clean, and use nature's own colors, fabrics, and graphics.

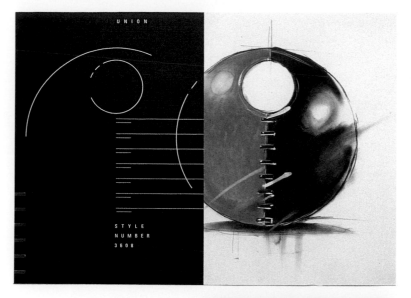

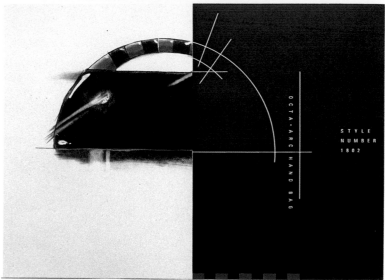

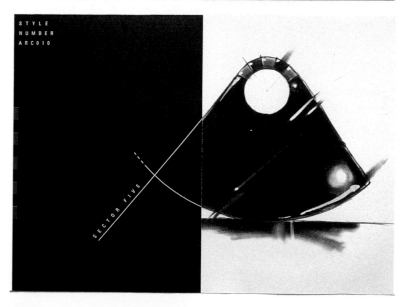

EC

THE REFLECTION OF TIME. THE
MILLENNIUM MESHED WITH ANCIENT
HOPES AND DREAMS. THE SKIN OF
INDULGENCE SHED TO BATHE IN THE
GENTLE WAVES OF UNIVERSAL
ANCESTRY EVER ETERNAL.

ECO — THE SPIRIT OF THE EARTH

EACH SHIRT DESIGN IS AVAILABLE IN DIFFERENT TEXTURES

KENCATO

Cato Projects

These books represent the philosophy and feel of Ken Cato clothes, which are designed to move with you and work for you in fabrics that perform. The format of the book reflects a style that never quits.

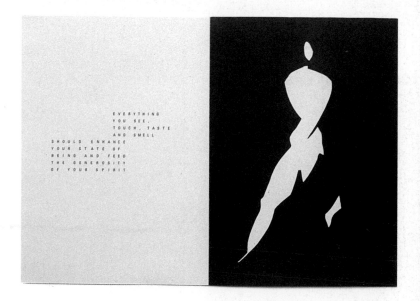